THE
PHOTOGRAPHER'S
EQUIPMENT
BOOK

THE
PHOTOGRAPHER'S
EQUIPMENT
BOOK

Michael
Busselle

WINDWARD

Windward
An imprint owned by
W. H. Smith & Son Limited
Registered No 237811 England

Trading as WHS Distributors,
St John's House,
East Street,
Leicester, LE1 6NE

First published 1984

ISBN 0 7112 0368 7

Designed and produced by Robert Adkinson Limited
Editorial Director: Clare Howell
Editor: Hilary Dickinson
Designers: David Fordham, Martin Atcherley
Illustrator: Rick Blakely

Phototypeset by Ashwell Print Services Ltd.,
Ashwellthorpe, Norwich
Illustrations originated by East Anglian Engraving Co. Ltd.,
Norwich
Printed and bound by Graficromo, Cordoba, Spain

Introduction

The amateur photographer today has a greater
variety of cameras, lenses and other types of
accessories available to him than even the
professional and specialist worker had a decade
or so ago. Because of this bewildering choice,
even the more experienced photographer is
often confused about the best choice and use
of a particular piece of equipment; the beginner
is completely at sea. This book is designed to
guide the reader through the complete range of
equipment, explaining the advantages and
limitations of each and demonstrating the use
for each item to its best effect. But the book
does not only deal with the technical aspects of
choosing and using equipment; it also shows
how each item can be used creatively, often
suggesting uses which may not be immediately
obvious. In this way, the reader can choose
equipment from the start which may be fully
exploited in use. All aspects of photography are
dealt with — from family shots to creative and
expressive images. Finally, at the end of the
book there are two quick reference sections:
the first deals with choosing and using film and
the second is a comprehensive equipment
glossary. The latter will not only open up the
obscure world of catalogues and instruction
manuals, it will also give the reader an instant
answer as to the best category of use for each
item described: an invaluable tool for any
photographer.

CONTENTS

CAMERAS

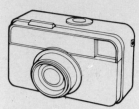

A cartridge-loading camera
using 126 film

Cartridge Cameras

The essential feature of a cartridge camera is that
the film is pre-loaded into a light-tight plastic container which can be placed directly into the camera,
thus eliminating the need for handling and threading the actual film, and making it an extremely
simple and quick operation. This in fact is the principle behind cartridge cameras – simplicity – as
they are designed to be foolproof, and to a large
extent they are just that. They are also intended to
be inexpensive, and although there are a number of
sophisticated models which are relatively expensive
to buy, they are all comparatively cheap to run,
while computerized processing means that the
small films can be developed and printed both very
quickly and very economically.

There are three main types of cartridge with three
corresponding cameras: the 126, the 110 and, most
recently, the disc. The main difference between
them lies in the size of the film and the cartridge
which holds it and the corresponding size of the
cameras. The earlier 126 cameras such as the
Kodak Instamatic are not a great deal smaller than a
compact 35 mm camera, but the design of the most
recent disc film and its cartridges has enabled these
cameras to be very small indeed, in fact a true
pocket camera.

The cartridge camera is
ideal for use with colour
negative film, allowing
inexpensive prints to be
obtained for family and
holiday records.

An effective way of using the small image of a cartridge camera is as a visual notebook. Its small size allows it to be carried at all times to record details of interest.

Simplicity of use makes the cartridge camera ideal for recording spontaneous moments with the greatest speed and the minimum trouble.

The simplified focusing and exposure control of a cartridge camera can make it easier for an inexperienced photographer to respond quickly to a potential subject.

A cartridge-loading camera using 110 film

With a few exceptions, such as the Pentax 110 SLR, cartridge cameras are designed as viewfinder instruments with a separate optical system from the lens, only providing a means of determining the field of view and framing the picture. This means that there is no indication of focusing in the viewfinder and the whole image is seen as equally sharp. Focusing is usually achieved by a simple 'zone' setting indicating head-and-shoulders shots, groups, and distant scenes. Because the film format is very small the lenses are of very short focal length, giving a comparatively great depth of field which is increased by the use of quite small apertures. In many cartridge cameras the lens is pre-focused at a fixed distance, leaving the depth of field to take care of both more distant and closer objects.

The more basic types of cartridge camera use simple symbols to set the correct exposure for sunny or cloudy conditions, with smaller variations in the light level being covered by the latitude of the colour negative film. More advanced models use a light meter coupled usually to the aperture to regulate the exposure automatically according to the level of brightness and the speed of the film. In most recent cartridge cameras there is a device on the film cartridge which sets the film speed automatically into the camera's exposure meter, and a warning or prevention mechanism to avoid shooting when the light level is too low. A further refinement of the more advanced models is a built-in flash and motor wind for the film, and there are a variety of other models with facilities ranging from built-in radios to digital clocks.

In addition to the main advantages of cartridge cameras – simple loading and operation, relatively inexpensive cost – they are also small and can be easily and unobtrusively carried around. Used within their limitations they are relatively foolproof and produce virtually guaranteed results of acceptable quality under the conditions for which they are intended. The main difficulty in using this type of camera is, in fact, their very smallness, particularly for someone with large hands, as they can be awkward to hold and operate. This is a point to

The small format of the cartridge camera means that it will perform best with subjects that are well lit and have clearly defined and bold details.

consider when choosing one. Because they are small and light it can be more difficult to hold them steady while exposing than is the case with a conventional camera, and care must be taken to avoid camera shake.

The main disadvantages of the cartridge camera can mostly be attributed to the small format. Although they will produce results of acceptable quality under good lighting conditions and when only quite small prints are made, difficult lighting conditions and greater degrees of enlargement will reveal their limitations. Even an expensive and sophisticated cartridge camera will not match the

To make the most of the small format of a cartridge camera, move in close to the subject and fill the frame. This will help to emphasize shapes, details and colours.

quality produced by an inexpensive 35 mm or roll-film camera when 8 × 10 in (20 × 25 cm) prints are made.

To make the best use of these cameras they should be kept within their limitations. Choose subjects which are well lit, with bold and clearly defined details, ensure that your pictures are framed quite tightly by getting close to your subject, and use the camera rather as a visual notebook where you emphasize the key elements of a scene rather than attempting to show the broad subject. It is best to rely on the visual quality of your images rather than the quality of the prints.

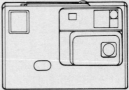

A disc camera

A 35 mm film cassette

If subject is close to the camera the lens must be accurately focused. A camera with a rangefinder or autofocus is the best choice here.

35 mm Viewfinder Cameras

To a certain extent, the 35 mm viewfinder camera bridges the gap between the cartridge camera and the more complex and expensive SLR camera since it provides a much greater potential for producing high-quality results than the cartridge but is still relatively inexpensive and simple to use compared to the SLR. The common factors are that the viewfinder camera uses 35 mm film in cassettes and that the camera is aimed by means of a separate optical system from that of the image-forming lens, as is employed in most cartridge cameras. However, the use of 35 mm film represents a considerable step forward from the cartridge; not only is there a possibility of producing better-quality prints because of the larger image on the film, but there is

A 35 mm camera gives you the option of shooting in black and white, making high-quality enlargements for reproduction and display.

also a much wider choice of films available. While the cartridge camera is suitable only for producing quite small colour prints from negative film, the 35 mm camera can be used to produce high-quality transparencies for projection, for instance, or black-and-white negatives for exhibition-sized enlargements.

Although the viewing method is similar in both the 35 mm viewfinder and cartridge cameras, focusing must of necessity be more precise in the former since the longer focal length lens required to cover the larger format of 35 mm has less depth of field. In addition, most 35 mm cameras have lenses with wider apertures which also limits the depth of field, and in order to obtain the sharpest possible pictures it is important to focus the lens quite accurately on the subject. In its simplest form this is done by setting the estimated distance on to the focusing mount of the lens, either using symbols or a scale in feet and metres. With practice this can be done quite accurately for most pictures, but at close focusing distances, say less than 2 metres (6 feet), this method can be unsatisfactory as the depth of field is much less when the subject is close to the camera. There are two widely used methods of overcoming this problem: the rangefinder, which is an optical device creating a double image of the

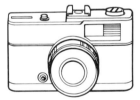

A 35 mm viewfinder camera

subject which merges together as the focusing mount is rotated to the correct distance, and the autofocus in which the lens is focused by a motor which rotates the lens mount to the correct focusing distance. The motor is activated either by an infra-red beam transmitted by the camera and reflected back from the subject, the distance being measured in terms of time, or by the visitronic method in which the correct focus is determined by measuring the image contrast as the subject is focused. In either case the mechanism is triggered by an initial depression of the shutter release and the whole operation takes only a fraction of a second, making it possible even to focus on a moving subject. The autofocus involves less effort than the rangefinder method but it does have some drawbacks. The infra-red method works well in all lighting conditions but the measurement is made from only a small central portion of the viewfinder so care must be taken when the subject is placed off-centre in the picture or when there are foreground details between the camera and the main subject. The visitronic method does not perform well when the light level is low. The rangefinder, on the other hand, is considered to be one of the most reliable and accurate methods of focusing, and in poor light can even be preferable to the SLR system. It is generally fitted to the more expensive versions of the viewfinder camera such as the Leica where it can be used with interchangeable lenses of different focal lengths.

The main disadvantage of the viewfinder camera in terms of focusing is that, unlike the SLR, the effects of the focusing cannot actually be *seen* in the viewfinder, so that regardless of where the image is focused the entire picture appears equally sharp. This can be a problem, for example, when judging the effects of a background. To some extent this is overcome by the depth of field scale provided on the focusing mount of most viewfinder cameras, which enables you to read off the area of sharp focus in front of and behind the subject upon which you have focused according to the aperture being used.

Exposure control ranges from very simple to fully automatic versions. In the simple type, an exposure

Unlike the smaller cartridge formats, the 35 mm camera is capable of producing colour transparencies that can be projected or used to make large-sized colour prints.

A 35 mm viewfinder camera with rangefinder focusing

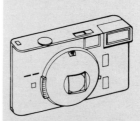

A viewfinder camera with symbol focusing

When the main subject of the picture is outside the central zone from which the distance measurement is made, as here, autofocus cameras are not recommended.

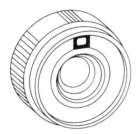

The light-sensitive cell on a viewfinder camera is usually positioned close to the lens so that filters cover both lens and cell. This makes exposure compensation for the filter unnecessary.

meter is used to determine the light level and corresponding exposure and is then set manually on to the aperture and shutter speed dials of the camera. With the fully automatic version the film speed is set on to the camera and a built-in exposure meter regulates either the aperture or the shutter speed (or both) according to the brightness of the subject. Unlike the SLR the majority of viewfinder cameras do not measure the exposure through the camera lens (known as TTL metering), but have a separate window. Other quite common refinements of this type of camera include motor wind to transport the film and re-set the shutter, and built-in flash. Most viewfinder cameras have a fixed lens, usually of between 40 mm and 50 mm providing a field of view of about 45%, but there are some models, such as the Leica M4 and Minolta CL, which have interchangeable lenses offering wide-angle and telephoto effects. On these lenses the different field of view is shown either as supplementary lines in the viewfinder or with the aid of a separate viewfinder.

The main advantages of the viewfinder camera compared to the SLR type are that in general it is smaller, lighter, less complex and less expensive. The disadvantage is that it is less adaptable and the choice of accessories is more limited. However, even a simple model will provide a definite improvement in the quality of results compared to a cartridge camera, and apart from having to load the film it is no more difficult to use, especially the automatic type. The viewfinder camera will enable pictures to be taken under more varied lighting conditions, while the greater image quality will allow you to shoot subjects with more subtle detail.

Although automation can offer a greater simplicity of operation it can ultimately become limiting, and so it is worth bearing this in mind before choosing which type of camera to buy. A camera with a wide range of shutter speeds and apertures which can be selected at will allows you more scope with your photography, and although a built-in flash can be useful for snapshots a camera with a facility for a separate flash-gun will allow you to use more effective ways of lighting with flash.

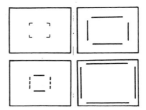

Lines showing the fields of view of different lenses in the viewfinder camera.

A camera with rangefinder focusing can be easier to use with poorly lit subjects as it can produce a more positive image than a focusing screen and, in addition, some autofocus systems do not operate well in low light conditions.

35 mm SLR Cameras

The design of the single lens reflex (SLR) camera gives it many advantages over the viewfinder type, and for this reason the 35 mm SLR has become the standard camera for both the keen amateur photographer and the professional. The essential feature of this camera is that the image formed by the camera lens is diverted by a mirror from its path towards the film up on to a screen where it can be viewed and focused with the aid of a pentaprism. This means that the same lens is used for both viewing the image and exposing the film, which allows the subject to be seen exactly as it will appear in the photograph. When the shutter release is pressed the mirror flips up out of the way, the lens automatically stops down to a pre-set aperture, and the shutter is released, allowing the image to record on the film. The mirror then immediately returns to its former position. All of this only takes a fraction of a second so that when a normal shutter speed of, say, 1/125 sec is used you only experience a brief flicker of interruption to the image you view on the screen.

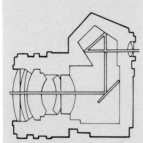

This diagram shows the light path of a 35 mm SLR camera

A further advantage of the SLR system is that whatever lens is fitted to the camera, the view on the screen will always be an accurate impression of the field of view. Most SLR cameras are designed to accommodate interchangeable lenses and there is a wide variety available for even the most inexpensive models. When a separate lens is used for viewing, as in a viewfinder camera or a twin lens reflex, the viewpoint of the taking lens is slightly different from the viewfinder and this can cause what is known as parallax error, i.e. the change of effect you see when you view a scene first through one eye and then the other. This problem does not occur with an SLR, which makes it particularly suitable for close-up pictures and when precise alignment of a subject is needed. Another very useful effect is that since you are viewing the image through the camera lens you will also see the effect of any attachments, such as filters.

The exposure system of the SLR also benefits from its design since the meter can be incorporated inside the camera enabling the reading to be made

The lack of parallax error in the viewing system of an SLR camera and its accuracy of focusing makes it ideal for close-up subjects.

from the actual image formed by the camera lens. This is more accurate than the separate window method used by most viewfinder cameras and will also take into account any filters or attachments used on the lens. Most modern SLR cameras have either semi-automatic or fully automatic exposure control. With the semi-automatic control, the film speed in use is set on the camera and then to select either a shutter speed or an aperture the correct exposure can be set by adjusting either the shutter speed or the aperture (or both) until a needle is centred or a light-emitting diode (LED) is illuminated. In the fully automatic version, the camera will automatically set either the aperture or shutter speed (or both) according to the film speed and the brightness of the subject. There are a number of choices available with automatic exposure control, some models offer all of them and are known as multi-mode cameras, whereas others use just one method.

A 35 mm SLR camera

Aperture priority means that you set the aperture, and the film speed, and the camera will select the correct shutter speed according to the brightness of the image. Shutter priority is the opposite: you select the shutter speed and the camera sets the aperture automatically. Programmed exposure control means that the camera will select both the aperture and shutter speed according to the conditions, and this facility makes an SLR as quick and easy to use as a cartridge camera in terms of exposure. A further refinement of some automatic metering systems is that they can be used to control flash exposures when coupled with the correct flash-gun; this is known as dedicated flash, and the duration of the flash is regulated by the meter inside the camera. With most of these systems there is a read-out on the screen which informs you which settings have been selected – there are a variety of ways in which this is done. Each of the systems has its own advantages: shutter priority, for example, is ideal for action pictures where it is important to select a fast shutter speed, whereas if depth of field is an important factor, in a close-up shot perhaps, it would be more useful to be able to select the smallest aperture given the light conditions.

Some means of controlling the exposure, such as a manual override or a memory lock, is vital for a picture like this which is shot into the light. Used in the purely automatic mode this picture would be under-exposed.

An exposure meter, of whatever type, will obviously only give the correct exposure under particular conditions, and in many cases the exposure reading must be modified: for example, when shooting into the light the normal TTL meter will tend to produce an under-exposed result. For this reason automatic systems incorporate a dial control which can be used to increase or decrease the exposure indicated by the meter, usually in increments of a third of a stop. If your camera does not have this facility you can achieve the same effect by altering the film speed dial: when using an ISO 100/21 film, for example, if you set the dial to ISO 50/18 you will over-expose by one stop, and by setting it to ISO 200/24 you will under-expose by one stop (remember to re-set the dial correctly after that particular picture has been exposed). Another method of controlling automatic exposures is with the aid of a memory lock. If, for instance, you are taking a landscape picture with a large area of sky the meter will be misled into under-exposing the film, but if you aim the camera down to get a reading avoiding the sky you can use the memory lock to hold the setting while you frame the shot again for the exposure.

Since SLR cameras are designed to be viewed and focused with the lens at full aperture it is not possible to see the effects of depth of field although it can be measured by the scale on the focusing

Depth of field is an important consideration for this type of picture if sharp detail in both foreground and distance are to be obtained. Aperture priority would therefore be the best choice.

mount in the same way as with a viewfinder camera. Some models are fitted with a depth of field preview button which enables the lens to be stopped down manually to the selected aperture; this can be very useful if you are taking pictures where depth of field is an important factor, such as close-up shots.

Another feature which is not common to all SLRs is a mirror lock. This is a device which enables the mirror to be locked up into the taking position, after framing and focusing, prior to releasing the shutter. When the mirror is released it causes a certain amount of vibration, which under some circumstances can produce unsharp pictures (when using slow shutter speeds, for instance, or with long-focus lenses or close-up shots), and using the mirror lock will eliminate this risk. However, as you are no longer able to see through the viewfinder it is necessary to shoot with the camera mounted on a tripod so that it does not move after being framed and focused.

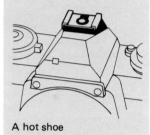

A hot shoe

A self-timer device is fitted to most cameras and, while its primary function is to enable the photographer to be included in a shot, it can also be used effectively in some circumstances in place of a cable release when the camera is on a tripod to avoid jarring when shooting at slow shutter speeds.

With most cameras, including viewfinder and rollfilm models, the film has to be wound on in order to re-set the shutter for the next exposure. This is primarily to prevent unintentional double exposures, but combining two or more images on the same piece of film can also be used as an effective creative technique. Although it is possible to do this by running the film through the camera twice, it is much easier with a camera fitted with a multiple exposure device which disengages the film wind from the shutter setting mechanism.

Many SLR cameras have a hot shoe which enables the camera to make direct electrical contact with the correct flash-gun when it is fitted, without the need for a flash synchronization cable. This means, however, that the flash-gun must be attached to the camera, which is often not the most effective method. If you wish to make full use of flash lighting it is best to select a camera which also

The faster shutter speeds of a focal-plane shutter can be an advantage when photographing moving subjects to obtain maximum image sharpness.

The mirror lock fitted to some SLR cameras can be helpful with subjects like this which require the use of a long-focus lens and a slow shutter speed.

has a normal socket for a sync lead. Most SLR cameras are fitted with focal plane shutters rather than the leaf shutters common to most viewfinder cameras; these have the advantage of faster top speeds and also make lenses less expensive since they do not have to be fitted with individual shutters. However, they have the disadvantage that they will not synchronize with electronic flash at all shutter speeds – usually at about 1/60 sec or slower – and this can be a problem when shooting action pictures with flash, for example, or when combining flash with daylight. However, some cameras

A camera with interchangeable lenses enables you to obtain a variety of effects by the use of lenses with different focal lengths. This picture was taken using a wide-angle lens.

will synchronize at faster shutter speeds – 1/125 or 1/250 sec – and if you intend to use flash under these conditions, select one of these.

When deciding whether to buy an SLR in preference to a viewfinder camera, the main consideration must be whether you will require additional lenses; although some 35 mm viewfinder cameras have this facility the SLR offers a far wider range and is really the obvious choice. What possible advantages would an SLR have, then, for the photographer who who does not want extra lenses? Its viewfinder gives more accurate impression of the way the final photograph will appear, which can be a useful aid to composition, and the effects of filters and other attachments can be much more readily seen and controlled. Most SLRs have faster shutter speeds than the viewfinder type and for this reason are more suitable for fast-moving subjects; the limit of most leaf shutters is 1/500 sec, while 1/1000 sec is commonplace with focal plane shutters and some cameras offer a top speed of up to 1/4000 sec. The SLR is a much better choice for subjects close to the camera since there is not the problem of parallax error which exists with the viewfinder type, and close-up attachments are also available for use only with cameras with detachable lenses. It is also important to appreciate that the scope of even a modestly priced SLR can be expanded by the addition of accessories to cope with a wider range of subjects than most 35 mm viewfinder cameras (with the exception of a few instruments, such as the

Quite a different effect has been created in this picture by using a long-focus lens.

Leica, the viewfinder 35 mm cannot be considered as a system camera). As regards the disadvantages of the SLR where additional lenses are not required, the most obvious difference is that the SLR tends to be larger and heavier than the viewfinder, although there is now a trend to produce similarly compact SLRs at the lower end of the price scale. Viewfinder cameras are quieter in operation, however, and cameras such as the Leica are often the best choice where this can be a consideration, such as theatre or reportage work, where the SLR can be too intrusive. Although optically there will be nothing to choose between two types of camera of comparable quality, the very nature of the metering systems tends to make the SLR more accurate over a wider range of lighting conditions. In sum, if you feel that you are likely to want to take your photography a stage beyond that of casual and occasional use, then an SLR might well be preferable.

Rollfilm Cameras

Just as the 35 mm format offers a significant improvement in image quality over the cartridge camera, so the rollfilm format enables a similar improvement to be gained over 35 mm, and although many exponents of the 35 mm system will argue that results of comparable quality can be obtained by the use of careful technique and slow films, this is not really so. There is an old adage among photographers when discussing negatives (or transparencies) that a good big one will always beat a good little one. When you consider that to make an 8×10 inch print from a 35 mm negative requires an enlargement of 8 times, and a print from, say, a 2¼ inch square negative only requires half that, it is obvious that the rollfilm format offers a considerable advantage. The difference becomes even greater when shooting under unfavourable conditions or when the images obtained are of less than optimum quality, and even more so when greater enlargements are made. Although it may be difficult to tell an 8×10 print from a top-quality negative or transparency made on a slow, fine-grained 35 mm film from that made on a rollfilm camera, the difference between two 16×20 inch prints made on a medium or fast film will be very marked indeed.

All this would imply that the 35 mm camera is inherently inferior to the rollfilm type and that the latter would automatically be the best choice; this is quite obviously not so, since a glance at photographic books and magazines will show that some of the best photography is produced on 35 mm equipment. This being so, when and why should a rollfilm be used, and what are the advantages and disadvantages of this type of equipment? The basic reason for selecting a rollfilm format is, of course, where the most important concern is the quality of the image, for recording fine detail, for example. In fashion photography, 35 mm cameras are quite frequently used for editorial features where the mood and style of a shot is paramount; by contrast, for an advertising feature in which the texture of the fabric and the detail and features of a garment are the main

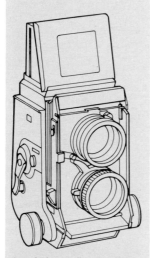

A twin lens reflex camera which produces 12 2¼ in-square pictures on 120-rollfilm

concern, it would be much more likely that a roll-film or even a sheet film camera would be chosen. Another important consideration is the purpose for which the pictures are intended: if, for instance, they were to be used for a poster then the larger format would be a more suitable choice, but for an audio-visual presentation 35 mm equipment would be preferable.

Professional photographers often use rollfilm cameras because the results look more impressive and because it is easier for the client to assess and select pictures from a sheet of 2¼ square contacts or transparencies than from 35 mm. This is also true at

It is often better to use rollfilm for pictures like this shot which was taken for a holiday brochure. They are easier to assess and can be enlarged more than those on 35 mm film without suffering any loss of quality.

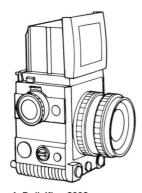

A Rolleiflex 6006 camera body

These three pictures demonstrate how the 2 ¼ in-square format can be used in such a way that the final picture shape can be determined after the pictures have been taken. The two pictures on the far left have been cropped to create a quite different composition from the full frame on the near left.

the time of shooting: an art director will often prefer a photographer to use a rollfilm camera because the image on the screen is much larger and easier to judge, and of course when Polaroids are used the rollfilm format is a much more obvious choice. Another consideration in commercial photography is that it is quite feasible to retouch a transparency of rollfilm size but very difficult indeed, and expensive, with a 35 mm shot. Negatives and transparencies shot on rollfilm also offer more potential for cropping than 35 mm. This is particularly true of 2¼ square, and many people use this format so that the decision as to the way the picture is cropped and composed can be made after the shot is taken; this can be a particular advantage when the photograph has to be combined with other graphics such as lettering or artwork. For these reasons, the rollfilm format is usually preferred by most photographic libraries, and photographers who would like to find an outlet for their work in this field will find it an advantage to use this type of equipment.

A viewfinder-type rollfilm camera

As regards the disadvantages of rollfilm cameras, they are in general more expensive than 35 mm equipment although a basic twin lens reflex would be less expensive than, for example, a top-of-the-

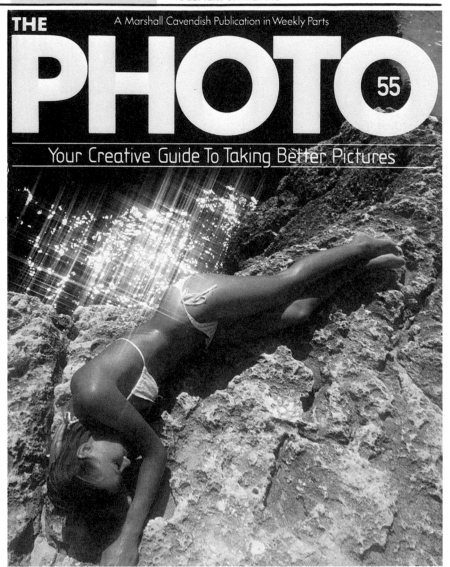

THE
A Marshall Cavendish Publication in Weekly Parts

PHOTO 55

Your Creative Guide To Taking Better Pictures

When photographs have to be combined with type, as in this magazine cover, the rollfilm format can be preferable.

range 35 mm SLR. Another factor is that lenses and other accessories are more expensive: a lens hood for a camera such as the Hasselblad could cost as much as a cheap lens for an SLR. On the face of it, they are also more expensive to run, with a roll of 120 film giving 12 exposures costing about the same as a 35 mm cassette giving 36 images. However, this is only half true since using a rollfilm camera tends to promote a more selective and sparing approach to making exposures, and in practice the difference in film costs may well not be as great as it at first seems. Another, practical, disadvantage is that rollfilm equipment is generally much heavier and bulkier than 35 mm, and for travel or reportage work this can be a serious drawback.

On a different level, because the 35 mm SLR is more widely used and is understandably more popular with the much larger amateur market, greater technological advances have been made with this equipment and the rollfilm camera tends to lag behind. Although automatic metering and motor wind are available for these cameras they are generally quite expensive supplementary extras rather than being built into the camera; one exception is the Rolleiflex SLX, which obviously represents a direction that rollfilm cameras will take, but it is likely that the 35 mm SLR will always be ahead in such developments. This is also true of additional lenses, where the range is much greater for 35 mm: extreme wide-angles, long telephotos and specialist lenses, for instance, are much more readily available in this format as well as being less expensive than their rollfilm equivalents. The rollfilm camera is also on the whole slower and more cumbersome to operate than a 35 mm camera,

Photographs like this one of the Maldive Islands, which are intended primarily for photo library use are often better when shot on rollfilm format.

especially when hand-held, and would not be the obvious choice where quick, off-the-hip shooting is needed, for sports or reportage photography, for instance; as a general rule, most rollfilm cameras are easier to use when mounted on a tripod although there are experienced users who might argue otherwise.

A final consideration when choosing a type of camera is style. Its suitability should be considered not only in terms of facilities and image quality but also in the type of picture that it produces. Most experienced photographers will agree that the choice of camera will also affect the way they approach a subject and will influence the visual quality of the finished image, and so they will also bear this in mind when selecting a camera for a particular assignment.

The choice of camera also affects the style and approach of an individual photographer. In fashion photography, for example, sheet-film, rollfilm and 35mm cameras can be used. Considering which camera should be used is as important as image quality itself.

The Twin Lens Reflex

The twin lens reflex (TLR) was for many years the standard tool of the general professional photographer, and the Rolleiflex was as common in these circles as the Hasselblad is today. Only a few cameras of this type are still manufactured and of these only one, the Mamiyaflex, has provision for interchangeable lenses. The camera is designed to produce 12 pictures of 6×6 centimetres on 120 film. The main advantage of the format is that it is relatively inexpensive compared to the rollfilm SLR and the main disadvantage is that it uses a separate lens for viewing purposes; this is situated above the taking lens and the image it creates is reflected up on to a ground-glass screen where it is seen reversed left to right. However, there is the problem of parallax error and for this reason the format is not as suitable for close-up subjects.

A twin lens reflex camera has separate viewing and taking lenses although, as in the SLR, the focusing and viewing are done on a screen. This separate action of a twin lens reflex can present parallax problems with some subjects, like in this picture for example.

Viewfinder Rollfilm Cameras

The large image on the viewing screen and on the resulting transparency makes the rollfilm format preferable for shots where the photographer is working with an art director or client present as it can be easier to assess the image more clearly, particularly when the pictures are to be used as part of a design or layout.

There are a number of rollfilm cameras which utilize a direct-vision viewfinder for image composition and a rangefinder for focusing. These are available to produce eight 6×9 cm images on 120 film, ten 6×7 cm, twelve 6×6 cm, or sixteen 6×4.5 cm; some models offer a choice of formats and some have interchangeable lenses. These cameras have the same disadvantages as the 35 mm compact camera when compared to the SLR design in that they do not show the effect of focusing in the viewfinder and they present the error of parallax. The only advantages they have is that they are lighter and less complex than the SLR. However, given the lack of thse two important provisions, they are not particularly inexpensive and are consequently not very widely used.

Rollfilm SLR Cameras

This is the most popular and useful type of rollfilm camera and is a standard item of equipment in professional studios as well as being widely used by serious amateurs. Like the viewfinder camera, the rollfilm SLR camera is available in a variety of formats – 6 × 6 cm, 6 × 7 cm and 6 × 4.5 cm – and in addition some models will accept a 35 mm magazine, 70 mm and sheet film, and instant picture film. Apart from actual image size, the main choice is between cameras with a focal plane shutter, such as the Pentax 6 × 7, and cameras with a leaf shutter, such as the Hasselblad 500 CM. The advantage with the focal plane shutter is that it provides a faster top shutter speed and since the shutter is built into the camera body the lenses are cheaper. The disadvantage with this type is that it

An SLR rollfilm camera with a pentaprism viewfinder

The use of electronic flash can decide the choice between a leaf or focal-plane shutter on a rollfilm SLR. A leaf shutter is the best choice where flash is used with daylight or when shooting fast action with flash, like this martial arts picture, as it will synchronise at much faster shutter speeds.

will not synchronize over the full range of shutter speeds as will the leaf shutter, which makes it less suitable for photographing moving subjects with flash and for electronic flash used in conjunction with daylight.

A waist-level viewfinder is standard on most rollfilm SLR cameras; as on a 35 mm SLR, the image from the camera lens is deflected by a mirror up on to a ground-glass screen where it can be

A rollfilm SLR with a rectangular film format and a standard, waist-level viewfinder, produces the image on the left: horizontal in shape and reversed left to right. By fitting a pentaprism to the camera, the problem of turning the camera to produce upright pictures is resolved and the image produced is reversed back to the correct form, as in the picture on the right.

viewed and focused. The image is seen the correct way up yet reversed left to right, but it can be reversed back to its correct mode by means of a pentaprism. This is in fact a vital accessory for a camera with a rectangular format as the waist-level viewfinder would be quite impractical when the camera is held on its side for an upright picture.

Few rollfilm SLR cameras have built-in automatic metering and this facility is usually incorporated into a special accessory pentaprism. Some models have a fully automatic exposure facility and, as with the 35 mm models, the choice can be between aperture or shutter priority. One of the major differences between rollfilm and 35 mm SLR cameras is that the former often have a facility for changing the film magazine in mid-roll so that colour and black-and-white shots can be taken of the same subject with the same camera very quickly and easily, while at the present time only one 35 mm SLR, the Rolleiflex SL 2000F, has interchangeable magazines. This facility also means that a separate polarized pack can be fitted to the back of the camera, for test exposures to check the composition and lighting, and then replaced with the film magazine.

Although the choice of lenses for rollfilm SLRs is quite extensive it is not comparable to the 35 mm

system; for example, lenses longer than 500 mm are rare for rollfilm cameras, and this is only the equivalent of about a 300 mm lens with 35 mm, and in addition many lenses for rollfilm cameras are much slower than their 35 mm counterparts, often having maximum apertures of only f5.6. A tripod may therefore be of great help.

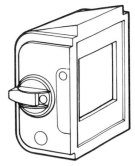

A detachable film magazine for a rollfilm SLR system camera

Sheet-Film Cameras

Large-format view cameras are relatively slow to operate and need to be supported on a tripod. They are therefore much easier to use with static subjects like in the landscape picture opposite.

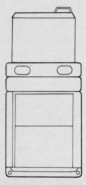

A dark slide taking one sheet of film on each side for use with a large format camera

For still-life subjects, like this arrangement of eggs, a large-format camera offers the maximum image quality to record fine detail and provides precise control over composition and focusing.

In terms of picture quality, the less a negative or transparency is enlarged the better the result. It follows, therefore, that the greatest quality can be obtained from the largest size of film available. Sheets of film are manufactured in two sizes: 8 × 10 inches and 4 × 5 inches. The cameras designed to take this material are quite different from other modern cameras and in fact have much more in common with the early plate cameras.

Large-format cameras consist essentially of a ground-glass viewing screen at one end, and a panel into which the lens is mounted at the other; the screen and panel are connected by a flexible bellows and attached to adjustable supports which can be moved backwards and forwards to enable the image to be focused. The image is seen upside down and inverted left to right. When the picture has been composed and focused, before making an exposure it is necessary first of all to close the shutter and the aperture down to the required stop. The film, which is loaded into a light-tight slide (one sheet on each side), is placed into the camera back in front of the ground-glass screen and the protective sheath removed; the shutter can then be fired to make an exposure. This procedure makes it almost obligatory to use the camera, mounted on a tripod, on fairly static subjects.

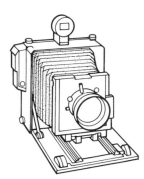

A sheet-film technical camera with a viewfinder

A flat bed or view camera taking sheet film

There are two main choices of camera design. One is the flat-bed camera in which the lens and film panels fold down on to a wide base into which the focusing track is set; this makes the camera relatively portable, and so this type is often used for landscape work. The flat-bed camera is often made in the traditional way in wood. The other design is known as the monorail in which the lens and screen panels are supported on a single base rail by means of tubes and clamps; this type of camera has to be virtually dismantled and reassembled for transportation and use. The advantage of the monorail is that it offers a much greater degree of adjustment, which can be very useful for certain subjects. Apart from the production of larger negatives and transparencies, the ability to adjust the relative positions of the film and lens panels allows considerable control over both the depth of field of an image and its perspective. Both of these panels can be moved laterally and vertically, as well as tilted forwards and backwards, and it is this facility that makes the large-format camera so valuable. Raising the lens panel, for example, means that the top of a building can be included in a picture without having to tilt the camera upwards, thus creating converging verticals, while tilting the lens panel forward allows both foreground details and more distant objects to be recorded with equal sharpness. The monorail camera allows a greater degree of control in this type of situation than the flat-bed design. A further advantage of the monorail design

These two photographs show how the perspective of an image can be controlled by the use of the front- and back-tilt mechanism on a view or monorail camera.

is that it is modular and some cameras of this type can be upgraded from 4×5 to 8×10 at a later date if required.

As the film and lens panels are connected by adjustable bellows, a wide range of lenses of varying focal lengths can be fitted to the camera and the focusing adjusted by means of geared wheels and track; however, for short focal length wide-angle lenses, it is necessary to use wide 'bag' bellows so that the lens and film panels can be racked close together. Although many photographers simply use a large black cloth in the time-honoured tradition to assist viewing, there are a variety of more sophisticated aids ranging from hoods with binocular magnifiers to a reflex viewing attachment which gives a corrected upright and lateral image. Lenses are available with built-in leaf shutters and automatic diaphragms, or a behind-the-lens shutter can be fitted for use with a variety of lenses, and it is even possible to obtain TTL (through-the-lens) metering with a special meter attachment, though obviously not automatic.

Other accessories for sheet film cameras include rollfilm backs which allow the user to shoot on 120 rollfilm, and also Polaroid backs for instant picture film. There are also special sheet film magazines for the 4×5 inch cameras which enable several sheets of film to be loaded and used in relatively quick succession as opposed to the conventional darkslide which only holds two sheets and must be removed and reversed to give the second exposure.

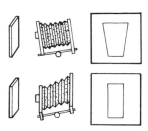

This diagram shows the perspective effect created when the camera is aimed down at a rectangular object and the way in which the converging verticals can be corrected by use of the front and back tilts.

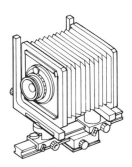

A monorail camera

These two photographs demonstrate how the effective depth of field can be increased, when photographing objects on a receding plane, by the use of the camera tilt controls.

Specialist Cameras

Most cameras are designed to handle normal subjects under normal conditions, but some designs, such as the SLR system cameras, can be adapted with the aid of accessories to cope with a variety of more exceptional situations and conditions. Apart from these, there are also a number of cameras which have been specially designed to overcome specific problems.

Wide-angle cameras

There are a variety of cameras made specifically for taking wide-angle pictures, ranging from basic wide-angle lenses mounted on a special camera body, such as the Hasselblad Super Wide or the Fujica GSW 690 (both taking 120 rollfilm), to panoramic cameras producing up to a 360° field of view. Most cameras of this type take 120 format film, but the Widelux and the Horizont are 35 mm cameras utilizing a rotating lens to produce a panoramic image. This type of camera is used mainly for landscape work, but at the same time it must be appreciated that because the resulting pictures are of necessarily unconventional proportions, the opportunity to use such pictures is much more limited. Consequently it is generally more satisfactory to hire a wide-angle camera for specific use; most professional dealers have these models available. The ordinary wide-angle camera is used for architectural and interior photography as well as

A 35 mm panoramic camera

This picture shows the extreme wide-angle effect of a panoramic camera which is achieved without perspective distortion.

landscape work, and some models are available with a perspective control or a shift lens; this enables the top of a building, for instance, to be included in the frame without having to tilt the camera upwards, thus avoiding converging verticals. This is a similar facility to that offered by a view camera.

A wide-angle camera with a perspective control lens was used to take this picture; the sides of the buildings have remained parallel as it was not necessary to tilt the camera up.

A wide-angle camera was used to take this photograph (*top right*) of Lisbon.

A Nikonos underwater camera

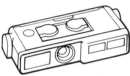

An underwater/weather-proof camera using cartridge film

A Minox miniature camera

A stereo Nimslo camera

An underwater/weather-proof camera can be useful for subjects like this (*bottom right*) where the rain and spray could damage a conventional camera.

Underwater photography

Accessory housings are made to fit a variety of conventional cameras for underwater work, but there are also a number of cameras designed specially for this type of photography. The Nikonos is a popular 35 mm camera which can be taken to depths of up to 50 metres (160 feet). It is a viewfinder camera but does not have a rangefinder, which means that focusing distances have to be estimated. It has interchangeable lenses and automatic exposure control, and there are a wide range of accessories available to fit the basic camera, including an underwater flashgun, which is vital for serious work. For more casual photography several simple and relatively inexpensive cameras are available, such as the Minolta Weathermatic which uses 110 cartridge film; however, these cannot be used at more than about 5 metres (16 feet). In addition to underwater use these cameras are also very useful for shooting in wet and rugged conditions where heavy rain or salt spray, for example, could be very harmful to a conventional camera.

Other specialist models

Other types of specialist camera include the subminiature models; these are instruments producing a very small image other than those in the category of conventional cartridge cameras. These include the Minox, an extremely small model which uses a special film giving an image of only 8×11 mm but of very high quality so that quite acceptable enlargements can be made; and the Tessina which uses reflex viewing and has a wide range of controls.

The stereo principle has recently been revived in the form of the Nimslo camera designed to make mass market stereo prints available which do not need the aid of a special viewer for their effect; the impression of a three-dimensional image is created on a flat surface by means of superimposed images taken through four lenses simultaneously. Another variety of multiple-image camera, such as the Cambo and Shackman, uses several lenses to create instant copies; these are used for passport, souvenir and medical photography.

Instant Picture Cameras

The subtle colour and image quality of instant picture film together with its 'one-off' uniqueness makes it attractive to photographers shooting fine art pictures and for personal and expressive work.

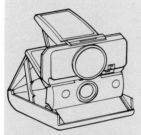

An instant picture camera using an SLR viewing system and taking single-sheet film

The introduction of the instant picture film by the Polaroid Land Company three decades ago has led photography into a new and constantly developing area. The basic camera, designed solely for the amateur, has now been extended to encompass a broad range of sophisticated instruments used widely by professional and specialist photographers. Instant picture cameras can be divided essentially into two types: those using peel-apart film and those using the single-sheet type such as the SX70. The latter gives a dry picture which is blank on emerging from the camera; formation of the image takes place in daylight by means of a chemical pod situated behind the surface of the film and activated when it is automatically ejected from the camera. The peel-apart film has to be separated by hand, and the surface of the print is initially tacky and must be handled with care until dry; the film also has to be pulled from the camera through the rollers which activate the chemical pod, and this must also be done carefully to ensure a good result. The advantage of the peel-apart film is that there is a wider variety of films and formats available, including black-and-white and a retainable negative, whereas the single-sheet film produces only a colour image. A further advantage is that, with colour film, the peel-apart image is fully formed after 60 seconds whereas the single-sheet film takes several minutes before the image can be assessed.

There are a variety of different models of instant picture camera designed for the amateur, most of them for use with the integral, single-sheet film. Although there are a number of quite different designs, the main choice is between direct-vision viewfinder types and single lens reflex. As with other types of cameras, the SLR models offer more precise viewfinding and focusing and are preferable for photographing subjects close to the camera. All instant picture cameras for amateur use have automatic exposure control so that there is no choice of aperture and shutter speed, but control over exposure is provided by a setting which enables the picture to be made lighter or darker. Both the SLR

and the viewfinder cameras are available with auto-focus mechanisms using a sonic beam. Some cameras have built-in flash and others will accept either flash bulbs or a separate electronic flash-gun. However, not all flash-guns are suitable for use with instant picture cameras and it is usually necessary to buy one designed for a specific camera.

The main disadvantage of the instant picture camera is that it is less satisfactory and more expensive where additional copies or enlargements are concerned, and of course transparencies are not available, as well as being more expensive per print compared to a cartridge camera, for example. On the other hand, being able to have the result almost immediately can be a big advantage, and additional copies of something like a souvenir photograph of a special occasion can be made at the same time and given to the people involved.

Although the quality of instant picture film can be very pleasing, the images are relatively small, and the best results will be obtained by framing the picture quite tightly and keeping the image simple and uncluttered, concentrating on bold shapes and colours and strong compositions. Many experienced photographers have in fact taken to using instant picture film for some of their more personal and expressive work, and the absence of a negative or master original lends such images a more unique and unrepeatable quality. This type of camera is also an excellent means of learning the visual aspects of photography – for a child perhaps – as the ability to see the result immediately will quickly help to develop a photographer's eye.

In addition to the cameras aimed at the amateur market there are a variety of cameras designed for the professional which take the peel-apart film packs; these are of the viewfinder type, usually fitted with a rangefinder for accurate focusing and in some cases with interchangeable lenses. Other types include cameras for making instant copies and multiple-image cameras for passport, social and record photography. It is also possible to buy Polaroid backs which can be fitted to many system cameras, such as the Hasselblad, as well as large-format sheet-film cameras.

Instant picture cameras are ideal for holiday and family record photography as the results can be seen immediately. Simple and tightly framed images make the best use of the relatively small prints.

An instant picture camera using a direct vision viewfinder

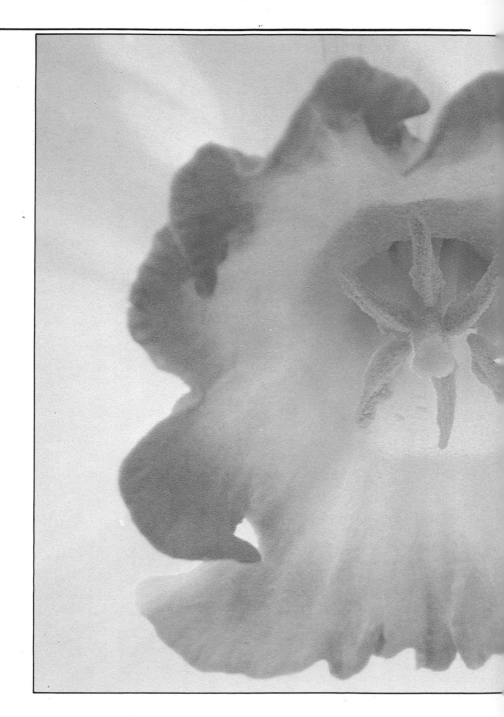

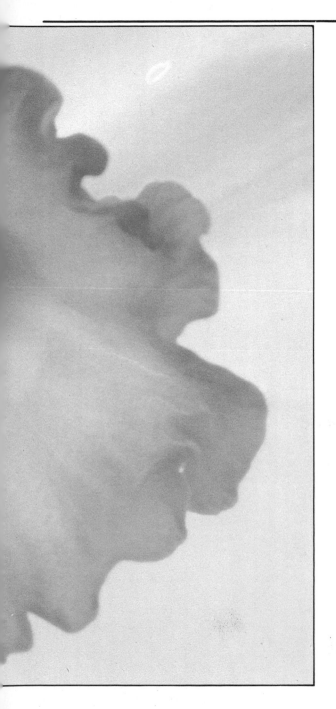

CAMERA ATTACHMENTS

Viewing Aids

A screen with a split image focusing aid

A screen with a microprism focusing aid

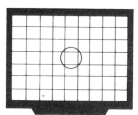

A screen with grid lines to aid image alignment

There are a wide range of accessories designed for single lens reflex cameras to improve and simplify the viewing and focusing operation, and one advantage of owning a system camera is that there is a much greater facility for adapting it to suit a variety of different subjects and conditions. With many 35 mm SLR cameras the ground-glass screen itself can be changed according to personal choice of particular circumstances. The standard type that is most commonly fitted combines a split field surrounded by a microprism and this is indeed a good choice for general work. Some subjects, however, are more easily photographed with an alternative screen: in architectural work, for example, it can be an advantage to fit a screen engraved with a grid of horizontal and vertical lines to aid perspective control and horizontal and vertical alignment. Very long-focus lenses are more easily focused on a plain Fresnel screen, particularly when they have small maximum apertures. A plain ground-glass screen can also be useful when extremely accurate focusing is needed under controlled conditions, such as in photomicrography or even still-life work; the disadvantage is that it is much brighter in the centre than at the edges, an effect which is accentuated when a wide-angle lens is used. A Fresnel screen with a large circular microprism in the centre is also effective for focusing and viewing in low light conditions, as is a full-frame microprism.

Although rollfilm SLRs are supplied with a waist-level viewfinder with a pentaprism as an additional attachment, both devices have their advantages and disadvantages under certain circumstances. A pentaprism is in general far more convenient with a hand-held camera, especially for following action, since it corrects the reversed image which the SLR mirror creates on the ground-glass screen and of course enables a camera with a rectangular format to be held as easily in the vertical position as in the horizontal. However, the waist-level finder can be far easier when shooting from a low viewpoint, for example; or when shooting directly down from a high viewpoint. Another

A waist-level viewfinder rather than an eye-level pentaprism can make shooting from a low floor-level angle much easier.

advantage of a waist-level finder is that it will allow you to place an overlay on the screen to assist the composition of shots where it is to be combined with type or artwork, for example.

Alternatives to the standard pentaprism and the waist-level finder include a number of magnifying heads which are available for some cameras and can be used for very precise focusing as in photomicrography. People who wear glasses can fit correction lenses to the eyepiece of some pentaprisms, and it is also possible to obtain high-eyepoint prisms in which the eye does not have to be so close to the viewfinder lens. A further very useful attachment for the viewfinder is a simple rubber eye-cup which, by excluding extraneous light, can make the screen image appear brighter and clearer. Another alternative type of viewfinder which can be fitted to some SLRs, and to viewfinder cameras if required, is a frame or sports finder for action photography when the camera is pre-focused and needs to be aimed quickly.

A focusing magnifier for use with a viewfinder screen

Motor Drives and Winders

A motor drive for rapid-
sequence use on a 35 mm
SLR

A motor drive can be a
valuable asset for action
pictures like this as it can
leave greater freedom for
focusing and camera
handling while allowing
rapid shooting.

At one time, these accessories were only available to
the owners of more expensive system cameras, but
they are now supplied as an accessory for a wide
range of models and are increasingly being incorporated into the basic design of a camera. The difference between a motor drive and a winder is that
the latter is a less expensive device which will offer
the facility of advancing the film automatically after
each exposure, and usually of also providing continuous firing of up to about three frames a second.
The motor drive, on the other hand, will allow a
more rapid (and in some cases, variable) firing rate
of up to about six frames a second in addition to
automatic winding. This accessory is invariably
more expensive and will only fit certain cameras
since continuous rapid fire requires a high degree of
durability in the camera mechanism in order to
sustain it. In addition to automatic winding,
making it possible to take pictures in quick suc-

cession, a motor drive also enables a photographer to maintain a more stable and constant grip on the camera and this can be particularly useful when using a long-focus lens, for example; it can also allow the camera to be held and operated with only one hand, leaving the other free to hold a flash-gun, for instance.

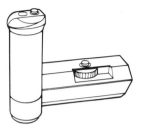

A motor wind for a 35 mm SLR

The use of an auto-winder can also make it easier to hold the camera in an awkward position: press photographers often hold cameras above their heads, for example, to gain a better viewpoint, and when combined with auto-focus this can give them a positive advantage in a crowded situation. The continuous firing mode is probably less useful than many people might imagine, and although it does 'hedge the bets' a little when shooting a rapid-action subject, unless a specific sequence of pictures is required it can be preferable to make the actual exposure by anticipation than by leaving the decision to chance. Even at six frames a second it is not possible to guarantee that a precise moment of action – such as a tennis-player striking the ball during a serve – can be captured by simply firing a sequence, and you are more likely with a good combination of good reactions and anticipation to achieve this by firing the shutter yourself. When a sequence is required, however, a motor drive is invaluable but it is important to appreciate that at six frames per second a cassette of film will be used in six seconds; to cover this, some films are available in special double-length cassette loads, and it is also possible to buy camera backs which hold bulk lengths of film.

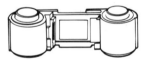

A bulk film back for use with a 35 mm SLR when a motor drive is used for continuous, rapid sequence shooting.

Some motor drives offer a rewind facility which can speed up reloading when shooting under pressure. Automatic winding is also invaluable for remote-release shots, when using radio control, for instance, or even a long cable release; a set-up like this is ideal for shooting pictures of birds feeding in the garden, for example, where the camera can be placed quite close to the subject and released from a distant, concealed position. An auto-winder can also add to the convenience of a camera grip and help to eliminate the risk of camera shake when using long-focus lenses or slow shutter speeds.

Releases and Remote Controls

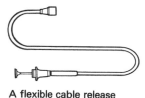

A flexible cable release

A long cable release can be a better way of shooting a self-portrait than the self-timer on the camera as it allows you to choose the exact moment at which to fire the shutter.

For most pictures, the exposure is made by pressing the release button on the camera body, but there are occasions when it can be advantageous to use a supplementary release. The most common device is a cable release; this is a flexible tube containing a metal wire which is attached to the camera release button, with another release button at the end of it. The advantage of this device is that its operation does not require direct pressure on the camera body itself and reduces the risk of camera shake. It is particularly useful for making exposures of more than, say, 1/60 sec when the camera is mounted on a tripod, and also for situations where camera shake is especially likely such as taking close-up shots or with a long-focus lens. In these circumstances, however, it will only be helpful if the camera is set firmly on a rigid tripod, and when an SLR camera is used it is also best to use a mirror lock to minimize the risk of vibration. Twin-shanked cable releases are available for use with extension tubes or bellows units not fitted with an auto-iris control; these operate the shutter on the camera body and the iris on the lens simultaneously. A cable release can also

Timid animals or birds can be photographed successfully by setting up the camera close to a predetermined haunt such as this bird bath and firing the camera from a distant, concealed position with a long cable or remote release.

be convenient for portrait photography as it means that when the camera is framed and focused the photographer can move away from the camera and will be able to devote more attention to his model; a motor drive can make this even more effective. Although a cable release is in some ways an optional accessory for small- and medium-format cameras, it is a virtual necessity for large-format sheet-film cameras.

Very long cable releases are available operated by a bulb creating air pressure. These can be used for taking a self-portrait by hiding the bulb in a hand or even releasing it by the pressure of a foot; this can be much more satisfactory than using the camera's self-timer, as the photographer can assume a more relaxed expression. A very long release can also be used for remote-control shots of timid wildlife.

A long, flexible release using air pressure

A much more sophisticated and expensive remote trigger can be fitted to many cameras which uses a radio signal to activate the shutter release from a considerable distance. This device is often used by sports photographers as it enables them to position a camera beforehand at a dramatic viewpoint – under a jump at a steeple-chase, for instance – or in some cases to have a camera at an alternative viewpoint – from both the bowling and batting ends at a cricket match, for example. In situations such as these both motor drive and automatic exposure control are of course vital.

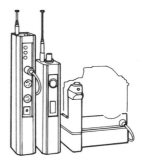

A radio-controlled remote release

A compendium, which can be adjusted very precisely, can be more effective than a lens hood when the sun or strong light is very close to the edge of the picture area, as in this shot of a waterfall. Alternatively you can hold your hand about a foot in front of the lens to shade it.

A lens hood

The effect of flare as a result of the sun being allowed to shine on to the front of the lens (*left*).

The improvement in contrast and colour saturation as the result of using a lens hood to eliminate flare (*right*).

Lens Hoods

Since modern lens design and production have improved the light transmission of lenses by means of multiple coating, the lens hood has become a rather less vital accessory, yet there are nevertheless situations where it is advisable to use one to prevent flare and the corresponding lack of contrast. The most likely occasion is when a bright light source such as the sun or a large area of bright tone like the sky is in a position where it falls directly on to the front of the lens. It is this that creates internal reflections and produces flare. A lens hood will exclude this extraneous light but will only be completely effective if the design is such that it shields the lens surface fully without encroaching on the field of view. For this reason it is best to buy a lens hood to fit a specific lens, preferably the one made by the lens manufacturer. A more satisfactory device is the compendium which is used by many professional photographers. This is a unit consisting of a bellows which can be racked backwards and forwards to match precisely the field of view of the lens in use. It can be used with lenses of different focal length with equal effectiveness as well as with zoom lenses for which an ordinary lens hood will be unsuitable at one end of the zoom range or the other. A make-shift alternative to a compendium for shots when the sun is very close to the picture area is to hold your hand or a piece of card some distance in front of the lens to shield it from the light.

When taking close-up head shots like this portrait of a child, an extension tube can be very useful as many long-focus lenses will not focus at a sufficiently close point.

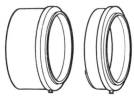

Extenion tubes for an SLR camera

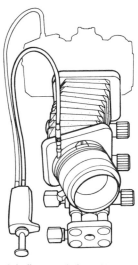

A bellows unit for a 35 mm SLR camera

Close-Up Attachments

One of the big advantages of the SLR camera design is that the viewing and focusing system makes it ideal for close-up photography, and there are two types of attachment which enable the ordinary standard lens to focus at very close subject distances. The least expensive of these are extension tubes which are available in varying widths, either singly or in sets of three or more. They are fitted between the lens and the camera body to provide different focusing ranges, allowing a small subject to be photographed at up to life-size or even larger on the film. Most extension tubes will still allow the auto-iris and automatic exposure control to function. In addition to allowing very close focusing with a standard lens, extension tubes can also be very useful when using long-focus lenses which often have a quite limited close focusing range. When taking portraits with, say, a 150 mm lens on a 35 mm camera or a 250 mm lens on a rollfilm camera it may well not be possible to obtain an image in which the model's head fills the frame without the aid of an extension tube.

When focusing at close distances the depth of field diminishes considerably as the distance decreases and it is often necessary to use quite small apertures to obtain sufficient depth of field. In addition, when using cameras with non-TTL metering both extension tubes and bellows units will require an increase in exposure to compensate for the distance the lens has been moved away from the film. This can be calculated by increasing the exposure by a factor obtained by dividing the square of the focal length of the lens into the square of the extended distance it is from the film. For example, with a 50 mm lens extended to 100 mm the factor would be $10,000 \div 2,500 = 4$, so the calculated exposure would have to be increased by a factor of four.

A bellows unit has the advantage that it offers a constantly variable focusing range as opposed to the fixed stages of extension tubes and this makes it more suitable for subjects where very precise subject distance or image size is needed, such as slide

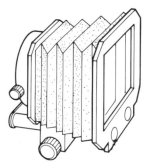

A compendium

An extension tube was used in this picture of wild flowers to allow the lens to focus at a closer point.

copying, for example. In general, only the most expensive bellows units allow the auto-iris and exposure controls to be used. When focusing on close subjects it is often easier to move the camera backwards and forwards rather than adjusting the focusing ring on the lens mount. With some bellows units the lens panel and the camera mount can be moved independently along a focusing rail, which makes very precise focusing easier; certain units also have a degree of tilt and rise adjustment similar to a view camera, allowing control over depth of field and perspective. As an additional accessory, many bellows units can be fitted with a slide-copying mount. It is essential to use a tripod with both extension tubes and bellows units to minimize the risk of camera shake and to aid more accurate framing and focusing.

This close-up shot of an apple was taken from only a few inches away with the aid of a bellows unit between the camera body and lens.

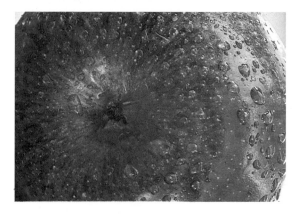

Copying Attachments

One of the most important considerations when copying a photograph or flat original is how to keep the camera perfectly square and parallel to the subject and also to be able to adjust the camera-to-subject distance. Although it is possible to make copies without the aid of a special attachment it is both more difficult and more time-consuming. The simplest and least expensive device for slide-copying consists of a metal tube which fits on to the camera body in place of the lens. The tube contains a lens of its own, set to focus on to a slide which is placed into a mount at the other end of the tube. Behind the slide is a piece of translucent plastic which, when aimed at a suitable light source, such as a tungsten lamp, electronic flash or daylight, will create an even illumination across the slide. Some copiers of this type are fitted with a zoom device which enables both the camera-to-slide distance and the focal point of the lens to be varied so that either

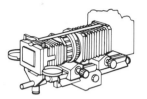

A slide-copying attachment for a bellows unit

A slide-copying attachment can make multiple exposure techniques like this picture of a piston much easier to control.

These two pictures show how a slide copier can be used to improve or change the composition of a transparency by enlarging and cropping.

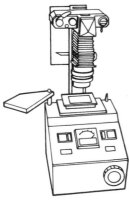

A slide copier for use with a variety of film formats

larger originals can be copied or smaller areas of a slide can be enlarged. If you own a bellows attachment you can also buy an accessory slide copier which can be used in conjunction with the bellows and the standard lens on your camera.

The most elaborate type of slide copier is essentially a light box which has a vertical column on which the camera is mounted and moved up and down to provide a wide range of adjustment. This device has to be used with either a bellows unit, extension tubes or a macro lens to provide the close focusing required. The advantage of this type of unit is that it has a constant light source so that once the basic filtration and exposure have been established it is relatively simple to adjust it according to the variation in the slides being copied. In addition, both the size of the original and the camera on which it is being copied can be varied, making it possible, for instance, to copy a 4×5 inch transparency on to, say, 2¼ inch square. This equipment exists for use with both artificial light and electronic flash; some models have built-in filtration.

Slide-copying offers a number of advantages. In the first place, it can obviously be used simply to provide extra copies of favourite pictures for friends or when you don't want to part with the original, for sending to a magazine or participating in a competition, for instance. It will also enable you to improve substandard pictures, for example to correct a colour cast on an original slide by copying it using a filter of the complementary colour to that of the cast, such as a blue filter to correct a yellow cast. It is also possible to make improvements in exposure errors: under-exposed slides can be made lighter and vice versa, provided the exposure error on the original is not too great. Even the composition of a picture can be improved by enlarging and cropping the original when making the copy, and unwanted details can be eliminated in this way. A slide copier can also be used for creative effects – small details of a picture can be emphasized, for example, by drastic cropping, and colour casts can be deliberately introduced to create mood and atmosphere. A further use is in making slide sandwiches or multiple exposures to produce a variety of interesting and dramatic effects; for the former, two slides are placed together in the same mount and are then copied on to a single piece of film, and for the latter, two or more slides are copied on to the same piece of film in the camera by the means of a double-exposure device.

Copying a print is much more simple and can be done quite easily without a special attachment, but for regular use a copy stand would be useful. This consists of a vertical column on to which the camera is mounted and aimed down towards the base-board which supports the print or artwork. The camera is moved up and down according to the size of the original in a similar way to an enlarger, and the illumination is provided by two lights placed at an equal angle and distance on each side of the base-board in such a way that it is quite even.

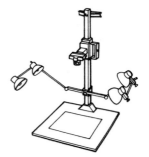

A flat copying set-up

LENSES

This picture, taken in very low light, shows the advantage of a wide-aperture standard lens; it also demonstrates how shallow the depth of field is at such wide apertures. Hence the need for accurate focusing.

Standard Lenses

Cameras are normally fitted with what is known as a standard lens, which means that it has a focal length similar to that of the diagonal of the film format of a particular camera; a standard lens for a 35 mm camera, for example, is usually about 50 mm, that of a 2¼ inch square camera about 80 mm, and for a 4×5 camera usually 135 mm. This relationship between the film size and the focal length of the lens gives a field of view of about 45° and the image produced creates an impression similar to that of normal vision. There are some variations, however, such as 35 mm compact cameras which often have slightly shorter focal-length lenses of 40 mm giving a wider field of view. With this type of fixed-lens camera there is obviously no choice, but with, say, an SLR there is often a choice of standard lens. The main variation lies in the maximum aperture; this is usually f2 or f1.8, but standard lenses with a wider aperture are available for many cameras offering f1.4, f1.2 or even wider in the case of the special Nokton lens for the Leica.

The advantage of a wide-aperture lens is that it creates a brighter image on the screen of an SLR making viewing and focusing easier, particularly in poor light, and it of course allows pictures to be taken in low-light levels without the need for slow shutter speeds. The disadvantage of the wider-aperture lenses is, firstly, that they are considerably more expensive and also larger and heavier, and in addition the more complex design and greater number of glass elements make them more prone to flare and some optical aberrations such as barrel distortion. The aperture settings also vary, with some lenses having 'click' settings at each stop but many having half-stop settings which can be much more convenient when working quickly and for bracketing exposures. The aperture numbers are determined by dividing the diameter of the aperture itself into the focal length of the lens so that in a 50 mm f2 lens the aperture would be 2.5 mm in diameter; this ensures that, regardless of focal length, the same f-number will allow the same amount of light through on to the film. The

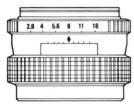

A standard lens showing the aperture

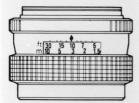

A standard lens showing the focusing and depth of field scale

These two photographs show the effect of aperture on the depth of field: in the lower picture, taken at wide aperture, only the post on which the lens is focused is sharp; the picture above, taken at the smallest aperture, shows both the distant and nearer posts equally sharp.

aperture settings are arranged so that each stop or f-number reduces the amount of light or brightness of the image by 50 per cent, so that f11 gives half the exposure of f8 and f4 twice the exposure of f5.6.

Most standard lenses will focus at closer distances than many other lenses – half a metre (about 18 inches) or so is common – and this can be a help in allowing semi-close-up shots to be taken without the need for additional accessories. The majority of lenses are marked with a distance scale in feet and/or metres and also with a depth of field scale, which shows how great an additional area of sharpness is obtained both behind and in front of the subject on which the lens is focused. This range of

sharpness (depth of field) increases as the aperture is made smaller and the point of focus is moved further away from the camera, and decreases as the lens is focused on closer objects and as the aperture is opened up. Some SLR cameras have a depth of field preview button which enables the lens to be stopped down manually, allowing the effect to be seen on the viewing screen. Cameras without this facility can often be made to stop down to the preset aperture by partially disengaging the lens from its mount. The depth of field is very shallow indeed at very wide apertures such as f1.4 or f1.2, and when used at these settings the lens must be focused very accurately to ensure sharpness in the subject.

Most standard lenses will focus down to only a foot or so allowing quite close-up shots like this paint-peeling door to be taken without the need for close-up attachments.

Wide-Angle Lenses

A wide-angle lens is one in which the focal length is substantially less than the diagonal measurement for the film format; with a 35 mm camera this would be a lens of 35 mm focal length or less, with a 2¼ inch square camera 60 mm or less, and with a 4 × 5 camera 90 mm or less is considered to be wide-angle. The focal length determines the field of view, so that while the standard lens of 50 mm creates a field of view of about 45° on a 35 mm camera, a 35 mm lens will create a field of view of about 62° and a 24 mm lens 84°. Essentially this means that from a fixed viewpoint lenses of progressively shorter focal length will allow you to include increasingly more of the subject and at the same time, of course, the objects within the image will be shown progressively smaller: a 24 mm lens, for instance, will show objects at half the size produced by a 50 mm lens from the same viewpoint.

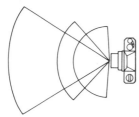

This diagram shows the fields of view of a standard lens, a medium wide-angle and an extreme wide-angle lens.

A wide-angle lens is in many ways the best choice for general photography when adding a second lens to a camera, since the effect of a longer focal length lens can be obtained by cropping and enlarging a picture taken on a standard lens but a wider field of view can only be gained by using a lens of shorter focal length. Another feature of wide-angle lenses is that they give effectively more depth of field when used at the same aperture as a longer focal length lens; this makes focusing less critical as well as enabling both close and distant objects to be recorded more sharply in a picture.

A further important aspect is that they can be used to have a significant effect on the perspective of an image. When we view a three-dimensional scene one of the ways in which we estimate the distance of objects and depth of a subject is by the diminishing size of objects as they become more distant, and the same effect occurs in a two-dimensional photograph. The relationship between the apparent size of similar objects, such as a street of houses, is a vital factor in creating the effect of perspective and the impression of depth and distance in a picture; this relationship is controlled by the viewpoint. If you look at two similar objects that are some distance apart, trees for instance, when seen from a close viewpoint the nearest tree will seem much larger in relation to the further tree and the effect of depth and perspective will be emphasized. However, from a more distant viewpoint the two trees will appear to be much closer to their

These three photographs show how a standard lens, a medium wide-angle and an extreme wide-angle lens (*top to bottom*) can be used in conjunction with a change in viewpoint to alter the perspective of an image.

actual relative size and the effect will be considerably reduced. It is this aspect of a picture which makes wide-angle lenses so useful; while it is sometimes said that a wide-angle lens distorts perspective, this is not so, and what it does do is to enable a photographer to choose a viewpoint that includes both very close and distant objects in the same picture, and it is this choice of viewpoint that creates the effect of depth and perspective, the wider the field of view of the lens being used the more this effect can be accentuated. This quality of a wide-angle lens can also be a disadvantage, however, as exaggerated or unwanted emphasis of this type can produce an unpleasant effect – a portrait photographed from too close a viewpoint, for example, can seem to distort the subject's features, making the nose and jaw appear too prominent, and a picture in which someone is standing in front of a distant view or place of interest can result in the latter appearing insignificant or lost.

The alignment of a camera is more noticeable with a wide-angle lens, so that when a camera is tilted up slightly to include the top of a building in a picture, for example, the verticals will appear to converge, giving the impression that the building is leaning, and similarly the effect of a tilted horizon in a landscape will be given more emphasis. In addition to the perspective effect, the ability to include more of a subject in the picture and the wide range of sharp detail made possible by the greater depth of field of a wide-angle lens can also create problems by making a photograph too busy or cluttered. For this reason it is particularly important when using a lens of this type to pay careful attention to the composition of a shot and you should ensure that there is a clearly defined centre of interest which is not lost or confused by intrusive background details.

Moderate wide-angle lenses

A moderate wide-angle lens, such as a 35 mm with a 35 mm camera, is often chosen by professionals involved in press or reportage work as an alternative to a standard lens. Its greater depth of field makes it ideal for situations where there is not time to focus carefully and its wider field of view makes it useful

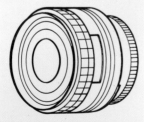

A medium wide-angle lens for a 35 mm camera

A moderate wide-angle lens such as a 35 mm for use with a 35 mm camera makes a good alternative to a standard lens for pictures of this type, the greater depth of field making precise focusing less crucial for quick, candid shots.

for shooting in crowds – often there is a large group of press photographers at an event and a wide-angle lens will allow an individual to get in front of the crowd and still include all of the subject. For the amateur, a 35 mm or equivalent would be ideal for family shots where there is some action involved: children on the beach on holiday, for instance, at a children's party or even a wedding, where the extra field of view and depth of field will be very useful but the perspective effect will not be so extreme as to cause undue problems. This type of lens will also be useful for landscape shots, allowing more foreground details to be included than with a standard lens and increasing the impression of depth and distance. Another use is for taking pictures where there is confined space or restricted viewpoint, such as indoor shots or in a street or market. However, if you are thinking of choosing a wide-angle lens of this type as an alternative to a standard lens, you will find that most have a smaller maximum aperture; there are some wide-aperture or 'fast' wide-angle lenses available but these tend to be much more expensive.

Medium wide-angle lenses

The medium wide-angle lens, such as the 28 mm on a 35 mm camera or its equivalent on other formats, offers a much more noticeable effect in both the field of view and perspective. Unlike the 35 mm lens, unless used with care this type of lens will give your pictures a more apparent wide-angle look. It is a lens which can be used in a similar way to the 35 mm, but the dangers of creating unwanted and unpleasant perspective effects are greater. At the same time, however, this lens offers more scope for shooting in confined spaces, such as the interior of a room, or for taking shots of buildings in an urban setting where viewpoints are limited; however, in these circumstances it is vital to keep the camera quite vertical as tilting it upwards or downwards will result in a marked convergence of vertical lines.

A 24 mm lens and a close viewpoint was used for this shot of a windmill to emphasize the effect of perspective using the lines created to make a strong composition.

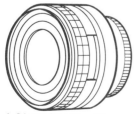

A 24 mm lens for a 35 mm camera

24 mm lenses

The 24 mm lens for a 35 mm camera or the appropriate focal length for a different format offers a compromise between the effects of the medium wide-angle and those of the extreme wide-angle lenses. It is wide enough to create quite pronounced perspective effects when required but can still be used in a less obvious way with a little care. It is also wide enough to be used for photographing all but the most confined interiors and is ideal for shooting architectural pictures where viewpoints are restricted, but precautions must be taken to keep the camera parallel to the building to avoid converging verticals. In some instances this will mean moving the camera further back to include the top of a building without tilting it upwards; this will mean that a large area of foreground will be included, and this can either be cropped afterwards or some interesting foreground details can be used to balance the composition. Another solution is to find a higher viewpoint such as from a window in a building opposite. These lenses can also add considerable impact to landscape pictures, allowing the inclusion of close foreground details in a distant scene, with the considerable depth of field enabling both to be recorded sharply. Dramatic skies can also be emphasized and the use of filter effects – a polarizer, for instance – will be accentuated. A wider-angle lens of this type can be very effective with pictures

A 24 mm lens has enabled quite a close viewpoint to be used, giving a fairly big image of the subject as well as including a large area of the background detail.

that contain strong perspective lines, a receding road in a landscape shot, for example, since it will increase the angle of convergence and create a more dramatic composition. It can also be helpful for the environmental type of portrait where you need to include a wide area of background as well as a large image of the subject and also, of course, an additional area of foreground interest in front of the subject.

A further advantage of these lenses is that they enable shooting so that the subject is unaware of the camera; this is possible because with a wide-angle lens it can easily appear to the subject that the camera is being aimed elsewhere while it is in fact including him in the frame. This technique is commonly used in reportage photography, and the degree of perspective exaggeration that can result is usually quite acceptable in this type of shot and can even contribute to the effect.

Extreme wide-angle lenses

Extreme wide-angle lenses, such as the 17 mm to 20 mm focal length for 35 mm cameras, can be used to create quite dramatic perspective effects and are often used for this reason alone. When photographing a building, for example, it can sometimes be effective to tilt the camera upwards in order to produce deliberately converging verticals, and this effect will be greatly enhanced by using an extreme wide-angle lens. Changes in viewpoint are also much more noticeable with shorter focal length lenses and when using, say, a 20 mm a difference of only a metre in the viewpoint can alter the composition very significantly. These lenses will help to emphasize the effects of a very low or very high viewpoint, and because both distant objects and details only a metre or so in front of the camera can be included in a picture, the impression of depth and distance can be greatly accentuated.

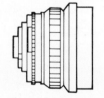

An 18 mm lens for a 35 mm camera

Another advantage of a lens of this type is for situations when extreme depth of field is needed; distances from only a metre to infinity can be recorded with equal sharpness if a small aperture is selected. When you want to obtain maximum depth of field it is important to bear in mind that the depth of field is greater behind the point of focus than in front of it – about one-third in front and two-thirds behind – so it is best to focus at this point rather than in the centre of the distance range. This type of lens is also of course invaluable for shooting subjects like small interiors where a longer focal length lens will simply not include enough of a room from the limited viewpoint available. However, they do tend to create a false impression of space due to the exaggerated perspective and the wide field of view. Manipulation of the scale of foreground and more distant objects is easy with extreme wide-angle lenses, and visual tricks are quite simple.

A 20 mm lens was used for this picture of an offIce building. It has greatly accentuated the effect of a low viewpoint and the tilted camera has produced a dramatic composition by emphasizing the converging lines.

Long-Focus Lenses

This diagram shows the fields of view of long-focus lenses

As its name indicates, a long-focus lens has a focal length significantly longer than the diagonal measurement of the film format with which it is being used; for example, a 150 mm lens would be standard with a 4×5 camera, but would be a long-focus lens when fitted to a 2¼ inch square camera or a 35 mm. A longer focal length lens produces a narrower field of view and at the same time enlarges the size of the subject on the film. A 150 mm lens on a 2¼ inch square rollfilm camera would give a 30° field of view, but on a 35 mm camera would produce a field of view of 16°. The degree of magnification produced by a long-focus lens compared to that of a standard lens can be calculated approximately by dividing the focal length of the standard lens into that of the long-focus lens; so, for example, with a 35 mm camera with a standard lens of 50 mm, a 200 mm lens would produce an enlargement of four times. As a long-focus lens also has an essentially much smaller depth of field than a standard or wide-angle lens, focusing must be accurate, and if sharp focus is needed either in front of or behind the subject then a small aperture must be used. Lack of definition when using a long-focus lens can also be caused by camera shake; because the image is being effectively magnified compared to a standard or wide-angle lens, so too are the effects of camera (or subject) movement and care must be taken to avoid this. In general it is best to select a faster shutter speed than normal, or to mount the camera on a tripod.

The main advantages of long-focus lenses are that they will produce a larger image of a subject without having to move in closer with the camera, and at the same time the narrower field of view will allow you to isolate small areas of a scene and to eliminate unwanted details. In addition, the shallow depth of field can be used to create more impact in a picture and to emphasize the subject. By focusing on the subject and using a wide aperture more distant background details will be thrown out of focus and the subject will stand out in bold relief. There is, however, another important aspect of a long-focus lens, namely its ability to control the perspective of an image: in common with a wide-angle lens, a long-focus lens allows you to choose viewpoints in order to manipulate perspective. The wide-angle lens achieves this by allowing both close foreground details and distant objects to be included, while the

These three photographs show how the field of view and subject enlargement are affected by using a standard lens, a medium lens and a long telephoto lens (*top to bottom*) on a 35 mm camera from the same viewpoint.

long-focus lens eliminates the foreground and concentrates the attention on the more distant aspects of a scene, in this way reducing the effect of perspective and diminishing the impression of depth and distance. The compressed planes familiar in sports photographs of horse-racing and cricket, for example, are a more extreme example of this effect.

The terms 'long-focus' and 'telephoto' are to do with the design of the lens. 'Normal' construction means that a particular lens must be at least as long physically as its focal length, while a telephoto design uses glass elements to make the lens more compact yet still retaining its effective focal length.

This picture of a cat was taken using a 105 mm lens on a 35 mm camera allowing quite a close-up image to be obtained from a more distant viewpoint, with the shallower depth of field creating an effective separation between subject and background.

An 85 mm lens for use with a 35 mm camera

Short long-focus lenses

The shorter versions of a long-focus or telephoto lens usually start at about two-thirds longer than the standard lens for a given film format, so that with 35 mm cameras it would be 85 mm or 90 mm, with 2¼ inch square 120 mm, and with a 4×5 camera 210 mm. Lenses of this type do not create noticeable telephoto effects and in many pictures it would be hard to tell that a standard lens had not been used. Their main purpose is in allowing a photographer to distance himself a little from his subject while still obtaining a large image, and for this reason they are used widely for subjects like portraits, children and domestic pets. In order to obtain a fairly close-up image of a subject's head when taking a portrait with a standard lens, it is necessary to use a close viewpoint, and the more unattractive effects of perspective can often be seen in such pictures with apparent distortion of the subject's face. However, a short telephoto lens will overcome this problem by allowing you to use a more distant viewpoint but will still create a quite close-up image. In addition, with many subjects such as children or pets this type of lens will allow a more comfortable working distance where having the camera closer to the subject could be disconcerting for the model. Even with full-length pictures of people a short telephoto can be an advantatge in creating a more pleasing perspective and also in helping to separate the subject more clearly from background details because

The effect of compressed perspective in this picture of an Andalucian village was produced by the use of a 300 mm lens on a 35 mm camera in conjunction with a distant viewpoint.

of the more shallow depth of field, especially if a wide aperture is used. In general, small objects will be more easily handled with a short telephoto, making it ideal for subjects like a still-life arrangement or flowers.

Medium long-focus lenses

The medium long-focus or telephoto lens has a focal length of between 135 and 200 mm on a 35 mm camera, and will show a marked difference in field of view, subject magnification and perspective in comparison to a standard lens. The 135 mm lens is also useful for portraiture, and since most have a quite close focusing facility will allow very close-up head-shots to be made without the need to approach the subject too closely. It has to be remembered, however, that the depth of field with such a lens is

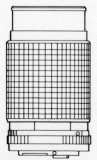

A 200 mm lens for use with a 35 mm camera

very shallow, particularly when focused at a near subject and so a fairly small aperture will be needed to obtain sharp focus from front to back of the point of interest. On the other hand, though, this can be an advantage since background details can be kept well out of focus, giving good separation to the subject. For this reason, this type of lens or its equivalent with a rollfilm camera is very useful for outdoor portraits and is used widely by professional photographers shooting glamour or fashion pictures. As regards studio work, its use is rather more restricted since apart from close head-shots there will have to be a considerable working distance between camera and model.

The medium telephoto is also very useful for landscape photography as it enables small areas of a wider view to be isolated and can create more tightly framed and selectively composed shots. The

This landscape picture was taken using a 135 mm lens on a 35 mm camera allowing a small area of the scene to be isolated which created a tightly framed composition and reduced the effect of perspective.

slight flattening of perspective which it produces can also help to give shots a 'different' look: although the impression of depth or distance is reduced the result can be an emphasis on the shapes, patterns and textures of a subject which can produce a strong graphic quality. When shooting sunsets it will give an effective enlargement of the sun itself which can also create interesting perspective effects with closer mid-ground objects. For distant views, however, a lens of 135 mm or larger on a 35 mm camera will tend to increase the effect of atmospheric haze, so a clear, clean light is usually preferable for this type of shot.

While normal perspective effects are reduced by the use of a long-focus lens an effect called 'aerial perspective' can actually be enhanced; this is the effect produced when atmospheric haze causes the different planes in a scene – hills and mountains, for example – to become lighter in tone the further they are from the camera. This type of lens can also be useful for sports and wildlife photography when it is possible to approach the subject fairly closely, though for more distant shots, such as arena sports, or photographing timid wild animals, even a 200 mm lens will be too short for most pictures. At these focal lengths the risks of both subject movement and camera shake are high and a fast shutter speed of 1/250 sec or less should be used whenever possible, and for static subjects, such as a portrait or a landscape, it is preferable to use a tripod especially as a smaller aperture is often needed.

This still-life arrangement was taken using a 200 mm lens with a rollfilm camera allowing quite a close-up image to be obtained without the need to have the camera too close to the subject.

Long telephoto lenses
A certain amount of both skill and practice are needed in order to be able to use a long telephoto of 300 mm or more on a 35 mm camera (there are few equivalents for the larger format cameras) since with smaller maximum apertures they are quite difficult to focus and the depth of field is very shallow

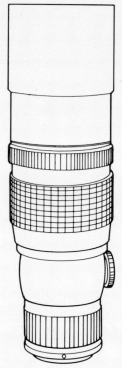

A 400 mm lens for use with a 35 mm camera

indeed. In addition, the risk of camera shake is further increased and so a tripod or some means of camera support, such as a monopod or rifle grip, is almost essential. The prime uses for these lenses are for sports and wildlife photography in situations where it is not possible to approach the subject very closely. However, they can also be very effective in landscape shots, allowing highly selective areas of a scene to be isolated from their surroundings. With a static subject like this it is best to use both a mirror lock and a cable release in conjunction with a tripod to obtain optimum sharpness, and it can also help to weight the tripod down, by suspending the camera bag on it for instance, to reduce the risk of vibration even more. Focusing on a moving object is very difficult with long telephotos, and for subjects like sport it is usually preferable to focus on a pre-determined spot and to make the exposure when the subject reaches it.

Mirror lenses

The mirror or catadioptric lens is an alternative to a conventional telephoto or long-focus at these focal lengths; its design uses a mirror to fold the light rays on their path through the lens, which means that it is much more compact and lighter than a long telephoto. This makes it easier to hand-hold, though it does not necessarily avoid camera shake, and in some ways it can be more prone to this problem since the bulk and weight of a normal long-focus lens can help to steady the aim of a camera. Most mirror lenses have a fixed aperture, usually of about f8, so the only way to control the exposure is by the means of the shutter speed or by using neutral density filters, and of course it is not possible to stop down further to obtain more depth of field. But they are much lighter, though their design tends to produce images of lower contrast and with some loss of central definition.

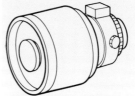

A mirror, reflex or catadioptric lens for use with a 35 mm camera

A long-focus lens is often necessary for subjects like wild animals and birds to obtain a sufficiently large image from a distant viewpoint. The shallow depth of field can help to separate the subject from the background as in this picture of a pigeon.

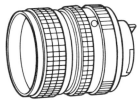

A 28–250mm zoom lens

Zoom Lenses

Zoom lenses offer two main advantages to a photographer: firstly they can replace a number of conventional lenses so that he has less equipment to carry around and also has to change lenses less often; secondly, and possibly more useful still, because a zoom lens has a continuously variable focal length (and field of view) within its range it can be used to frame a picture very precisely. Although a first-class lens of fixed focal length may have a slight edge in terms of image sharpness over a zoom, in all but the most exacting and critical work it would be hard to tell the difference from a good-quality zoom lens. One disadvantage, however, is that zooms tend to be somewhat larger and heavier than their fixed focal length equivalents and this can make them more awkward to use hand-held; this is particularly true of the wide-range zooms,

These three photographs show how the framing and composition of an image can be varied without moving the camera viewpoint by using a zoom lens. The picture above left was taken with a standard zoom, the picture below it shows the effect of setting it about midway through the range, and the picture on the right shows the longest setting of 210mm.

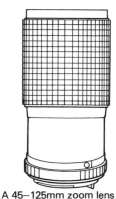

A 45–125mm zoom lens

such as a 70–210 mm.

A number of different ranges are available – a wide-angle ranging from about 25 to 50 mm, a wide to medium telephoto from about 35 to 85 mm, a medium range from 70 to 150 mm or 70 to 210 mm, and a few in the longer focal length from 200 mm to 300 or 500 mm. Landscape work is made easier with all zooms since the image can be framed exactly and unwanted details excluded by zooming-in. In sports photography too a zoom can be very useful as it allows you to adjust the framing of a shot as the action moves closer towards and further from the camera. Using the zoom during an exposure can also create interesting 'action' effects, as by altering the zoom from its longest setting to its shortest focal length as the shutter is fired streaks of highlight or colour can be produced radiating from a central subject. For this type of work it is best to use a fairly slow shutter speed of about 1/15 or 1/30 sec and it will be easier to control if the camera is mounted on a tripod.

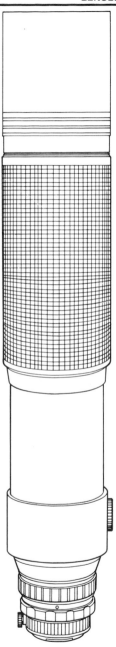

A 135–600mm zoom lens

Lens Converters

Lens converters are available as an attachment to an existing lens, either to shorten or lengthen its focal length. Attachments of this type affect the performance of the lens and unless a quite small aperture is used the definition will be poor. Wide-angle and fish-eye attachments are at best an inferior substitute for a prime lens of the required focal length, although a good-quality tele-converter matched to a manufacturer's own lens is a useful alternative in some circumstances. They are more satisfactory when used on a long-focus lens – converting a 200 mm to a 400 mm, for instance – rather than with a standard lens. However, a converter which doubles the focal length of a prime lens will reduce its maximum aperture by 2 stops, so that an f4 200 mm lens becomes an f8 400 mm lens, and you need to close the aperture down by one or two stops more.

A zoom lens is ideal for portrait photography, like in this picture of a clown, as it can be used to adjust the framing of the subject from, say, a head-and-shoulders to a three-quarter length image, without having to move the camera. This is especially convenient when the camera is mounted on a tripod.

A lens converter

These three photographs show how the image size, framing and composition of the picture can be altered by the use of a lens converter. The picture above left was taken with the prime lens alone. The picture above shows the effect of a 1.4 × converter; and below left, with 2 × coverter.

Specialist Lenses

An autofocus lens for a
35mm SLR camera

Autofocus lenses

In addition to the autofocus versions of the compact
cameras with fixed lenses there are now a number of
SLR cameras designed to take separate autofocus
lenses with a choice of both fixed focus and zooms.
Although much larger and heavier than a conventional lens, and more expensive, they do extend the
rapid focusing ability to users of SLRs, and given
the facility to shift focus automatically on a moving
subject they could be an advantage to those specializing in sports and action photography. However,
they have the same potential drawbacks as compact
autofocus cameras and, depending upon the
individual system used, can present problems when
shooting in poor light, with low-contrast subjects,
or when the subject is placed to one side of the
frame. It is also important to appreciate that there is
some delay in the time taken to make the initial
range measurement on the subject and for the
mechanism to set the lens to this distance, and when
a subject is moving rapidly towards the camera it
may move out of focus during this period.

Fish-eye lenses

These lenses offer a field of view of up to 180° or
more, achieved by a special design and configur-
ation of elements which produces an image in
which both horizontal and vertical straight lines
become progressively more curved towards the
edges of the frame. With a true fish-eye this creates
a circular image within the rectangle of the picture.
Semi-fish-eye lenses, however, are available which
produce an extremely wide field of view with
curved straight lines that fill the full frame of the
camera format. Most true fish-eye lenses are avail-

A fish-eye lens for a 35mm
SLR camera

able only for the 35 mm SLR cameras, but some
semi-fish-eye lenses are produced for use with rollfilm SLRs. In a purely technical sense, the advantage of a fish-eye lens is that it can provide a full
180° view of a subject (or greater), but in many
cases it is used primarily for its pictorial quality and
the ability to create strikingly unusual images with
strange and distorted perspectives, and with an

An autofocus lens can be useful for pictures like this. Shots where the subject is moving rapidly and unpredictably, need to be taken quickly with little time to focus manually.

This photograph shows the effect created by using a fish-eye lens: a 180-degree field of view creating a circular image within the film format.

appropriate subject it can produce effective pictures. The effect is so unusual, however, that it can easily become gimmicky if used extensively. For this reason and also because of the high cost of these lenses, many photographers prefer to hire them from a professional dealer for a particular occasion rather than buy.

Macro lenses

A macro lens is designed for close camera-to-subject distance with a greatly extended close focusing range, allowing a subject-to-image ratio of 1:1 without the need for other attachments. Many normal lenses, particularly zooms, are described as having macro focusing, but a true macro lens is also designed to give its best performance with subjects that are close to the camera whereas normal lenses are computed to perform best at more distant points of focus. In addition to close-up photography macro lenses are also useful for slide duplicating and copying, and when used in conjunction with a bellows unit or extension tubes can produce a wide range of subject-to-image ratios. They are available in both standard and long focal length versions for both 35 mm and rollfilm SLRs. The long focal length lenses are useful for maintaining a comfortable camera-to-subject distance, and some lenses of this type are

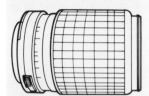

A macro lens for a 35mm SLR camera

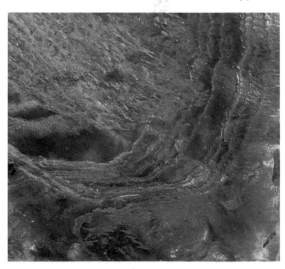

This extreme, close-up view of an abalone shell was taken using a macro lens fitted to an SLR camera, giving a subject-to-image ratio of almost 1:1.

made with a built-in ring flash to create a soft, even light and to enable the camera to be hand-held, designed primarily for medical photography.

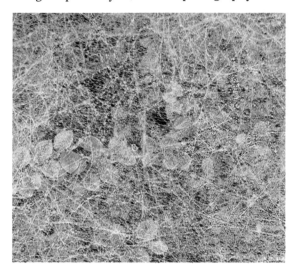

This photograph was taken with the camera about 8 inches away from the subject. A close-up lens was used to enable the standard lens to be focused at this distance.

Close-up lenses

Close-up lenses are attachments for a prime lens and are in fact weak positive lenses which have the effect of reducing the close focusing range of the camera. They are available in a variety of strengths, allowing the user to focus at progressively closer distances. Their advantage is that they are much less expensive then bellows attachments, extension tubes and macro lenses, and in addition they can be used on cameras with a fixed lens whereas the latter cannot. Their disadvantage is that like any other addition to the optical system of a lens they will adversely affect the performance with a noticeable loss of definition particularly at the edges of the picture, and for this reason they are best used with the lens set to a small aperture to minimize this effect. Unlike other close-up attachments they do not require an increase of exposure but it must be appreciated that when they are used with a view-finder camera with a fixed lens, the field of view will no longer be accurate because of extreme parallax effects and it will be necessary to allow for this when framing the shot.

Perspective control or shift lenses

These are essentially wide-angle lenses with a special mechanism allowing the optical axis of the lens to be offset, which means that the camera's view can be altered without it actually being moved. The prime purpose of such a lens is to provide a similar facility to that of the rise-and-cross movement on a view or monorail camera to users of 35 mm or rollfilm cameras, making them more suitable for dealing with subjects like architectural

These two photographs show the effect of using a perspective control or shift lens. The image on the left was taken with a standard lens; the converging verticals caused by tilting the camera upwards to include the top of the building. The picture on the right, however, was taken with a perspective control lens. By using the shift control, the field of view has been raised and the whole of the building has been included although the camera was held level.

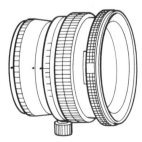

A wide-angle lens with perspective control for a 35mm SLR camera

photography. When photographing a building, if the camera is tilted upwards to include the top of a structure the vertical lines in the picture will converge towards the top of the frame. By keeping the camera perfectly level and adjusting the shift lens to raise the optical axis, the camera's field of view can be altered to include more at the top of the frame and less at the bottom without causing converging verticals. The same principle can also be applied when the camera is positioned to one side of or above the subject, so that a side or top view of a rectangular subject can be shown with its lines still parallel. The effect can also be useful on certain occasions with landscape pictures, for example, in situations where an area of close foreground is included in a shot; instead of tilting the camera down to achieve this, the shift can be used and the result is a subtle but effective difference. Even when the problem of converging verticals is not present, the shift lens can often be used to advantage to exclude unwanted foreground details, such as parked cars in front of a building, or to include additional area at the top of a picture such as an overhanging branch to frame a landscape shot. In this way a shift lens can also be employed to control the composition of a picture as well as the perspective. A perspective control lens can also be used

to create an interesting panoramic effect. Taking two pictures from exactly the same camera position, use the shift-control mechanism to move the lens in the opposite direction for each shot. Then join the resulting prints along a common line by cutting and butting them together.

Anamorphic lenses

These are available as an attachment to a prime lens and are used to create a wide-screen effect in projection similar to that of the Panavision cameras used in cinematography. An anamorphic lens is specially computed to create a laterally compressed image of the subject; when the resulting image is projected or enlarged through a compatible lens the compressed image is expanded to a normal appearance but giving a panoramic effect.

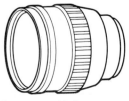

An anamorphic lens

EXPOSURE METERS

Exposure Meters
Types of Meter

Exposure Meters

With the exception of very basic models, most modern cameras are fitted with some sort of exposure control which is coupled to an exposure meter. In order to obtain the best results it is important to understand how an exposure meter works and in what ways the various types differ. The majority of exposure meters that are built into the camera are of the averaging type; this means that they read the light reflected from the whole of the subject area and indicate an exposure based on the assumption that the subject contains a normal range and balance of tones. For many pictures this will give an accurate exposure but by no means all shots are normal in this way, and this is when disappointing results occur. Exposure meters are calibrated so that if they read the light reflected from an even, medium tone of grey, the resulting exposure will reproduce that tone of grey on the film or the print. However, most subjects contain a wide range of tones from bright highlights in which there are no visible details, to dense black shadows; an averaging exposure meter assumes that if all of these tones were mixed up like the remnants of so many different-coloured paint cans the result would be the standard medium grey, and with a normal subject this will usually be the case and all is well.

On the other hand, an exposure meter cannot think and if it is pointed at a black object or a white object it will still indicate an exposure to produce the standard grey tone for which it is calibrated; in this way two close-up pictures of a white cat and a black cat would both appear the same, as a grey cat. Consequently, when the tones of a subject are abnormal a similar error can occur and it is important to know when a subject will create an abnormal average tone and how this will affect the exposure meter. When a subject contains large areas of dark tones or is in itself a dark-toned object, like a black cat, then the meter will be fooled into reading it as a standard grey and will indicate more exposure than is actually required, producing an over-exposed result. In a similar way, if the subject contains unusually large areas of light tone or is

With a scene of average tones, like this landscape picture, the exposure meter will indicate a correct exposure and the recorded image will match the actual appearance of the subject.

A normal exposure reading will cause underexposure in a subject inherently light in tone, making the photograph record darker than the subject appeared visually.

An exposure reading made from a subject which is inherently dark in tone, such as this portrait will result in an overexposed picture, making the photograph appear lighter than it should.

When shooting into the light, a normal exposure reading will result in an underexposed picture, causing it to record much darker than it appeared visually.

essentially light in tone, like a white cat, then the meter will believe it to be a standard grey tone and will indicate less exposure than is needed, producing an under-exposed result.

This will also occur with a subject that contains strong highlights, such as when shooting into the light or with night shots where the light sources themselves are included within the subject area. In such cases it is necessary to take the reading in such a way that the large areas of light tone or the very bright highlights are excluded from the meter's

TTL metering has the advantage that it compensates for filters and other attachments fitted over the camera lens, avoiding the need for separate calculations.

An exposure readout on the screen of an SLR camera with TTL metering

view. This can be done by moving in closer to take the reading, for example, or by taking a substitute reading by aiming the meter at a part of the scene which is more normal in tone but is lit in the same way as the subject you wish to photograph. With a fully automatic camera you will have to use the memory lock to hold the meter setting at the substitute reading while you re-frame the camera in the correct way and fire the shutter. An alternative is to estimate the amount by which the average grey is being altered – with practice this is quite simple, and many automatic cameras have a 'back-light' button which increases the exposure by usually one and a half stops, the amount by which shooting into the light distorts the reading normally.

Another method, and one which must be used if more or less exposure adjustment is required, is to use the film speed dial on an automatic camera. Setting the dial to a higher speed than the film being used will give less exposure than the meter indicates, and setting it to a lower speed will give more exposure; for example, setting it to ISO 100/21 with a film of ISO 50/18 will result in one stop less exposure, while a setting of ISO 100/21 with an ISO 400/27 film will give two stops more exposure. Many automatic cameras have a separate exposure compensation dial which enables the exposure to be both increased and decreased in increments of one-third of a stop up to plus and minus two or three stops. It is vital to remember to set both film speed and exposure compensation dials back to normal after the shot has been taken.

When using long telephoto lenses or ultra-wide angles, TTL metering will give a more accurate exposure indication than a separate meter would when used in the normal way.

The main difference between cameras which use average metering is that the viewfinder type is usually fitted with a meter which reads through a separate window from that of the camera lens, whereas the SLR camera is fitted with a meter inside the camera body and makes the reading through the lens. The latter tends to be more accurate and has the added advantage of automatically adjusting the area of the reading according to the lens or lens attachments being used. In addition, through-the-lens (TTL) metering enables the meter to be biased so that it is usually influenced more by the central area of the viewfinder than the perimeters, because this is where the main point of interest is usually placed; this is known as centre-weighted metering and is most frequently used in SLR cameras. However, this method will not give the most accurate result when the subject is placed to one side of the frame or if a centrally placed subject is dark or light in tone, so you will still have to consider the nature and tone of the subject before taking a reading.

The light path of a 35mm SLR camera with TTL metering

Another less common variation of TTL metering is spot metering where the reading is taken from a very small area of the subject indicated on the screen. This enables a reading to be made from a very precise area of tone within the subject, usually from something which approximates to the standard grey tone. Alternatively it can be used to make a reading from both the lightest and darkest tones in which detail is required and to calculate the average exposure which will record these both satisfactorily.

Types of Meter

Hand meters

Before TTL metering was generally adopted, the standard method of exposure calculation, and one that is still common among professional photographers, is the use of a separate hand meter. Although this type of meter cannot be aimed with the same accuracy as a TTL meter it is none the less advantageous in some circumstances. It can be particularly useful, for example, when working with a tripod-mounted camera; with a subject like a portrait it is much easier to take a close-up reading from the subject with a hand meter than it would be to have to move a camera with a TTL meter. With some cameras lacking this facility, such as a view camera for example, a hand meter is obviously a necessity. A further advantage is that most hand

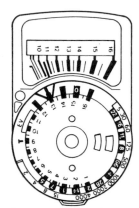

An exposure meter for reading both incident and reflected light

A separate meter can be very useful for taking close-up readings of a subject, like a portrait, or for taking incident light readings.

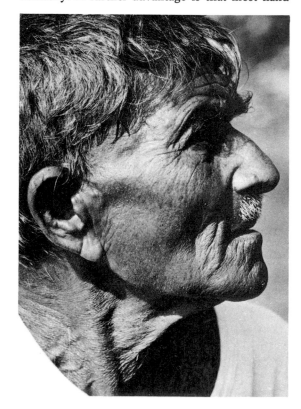

meters can be adapted to take incident light readings as well as reflected light readings; with the
latter, the meter has to be aimed at the subject
from the camera position to measure the light
reflected from it, but an incident light reading is
taken from the subject position to measure the light
falling on it. This method can be much more
accurate with subjects of an abnormal tonal range or
when the subject is very light or dark in tone, and
when using a multiple lighting arrangement an
incident meter can be used to measure the brightness of individual sources in order to adjust the
balance between them. For difficult lighting situations, such as high contrast, it is possible to
combine both reflected and incident light reading
for a more accurate result. A final advantage of the
hand-held meter is that in the event of a fault or a
breakdown, the camera itself is not put out of
action.

Spot meters

These are a variation of the ordinary hand meter
with the difference that they read from a very
narrow field of view – whereas the conventional
meter reads from about a 45° field of view, the spot
meter can read from as little as 1°, enabling a reading to be taken from a very small and precise area of
the subject. The spot meter is aimed by means of a
lens and a viewing screen with the area being
measured marked on it. This type of meter is ideal
for taking selective readings when it is not possible
to approach the subject closely, and it can also be
very effective when using long-focus lenses with a
non-TTL camera. A further advantage is that a spot
meter can be used to measure the brightness range
or contrast of a subject, by taking a reading from
both the brightest and darkest tones and calculating
the difference between them. In this way it is possible to determine whether the contrast is within the
tolerance of the film, and if not, the exposure can be
calculated so that detail is retained in the most
important areas. A spot meter is also invaluable if
you are using the zone system of exposure calculation in which the tonal range of a subject is divided
into equal steps on a grey scale, each representing a
one-stop difference in density and brightness.

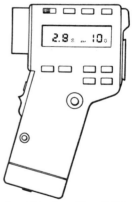

A spot meter with a digital
display

An exposure meter for electronic flash

This diagram shows how to read reflected light (left) and incident light (right) with an exposure meter.

A flash meter is vital for exposure calculations when using electronic flash in the studio as a normal exposure meter will not register.

Flash meters

A different type of exposure meter is required for use with electronic flash, because a normal exposure meter measures only the intensity of the light whereas a flash exposure is determined by the duration of the flash as well as its intensity. Most meters of this type are designed to take incident light readings and are either synchronized to the flash so that the flash can be fired by the meter from the subject position or the meter can be placed in position and the flash fired manually. Most flash meters now use a digital or LED indication of exposure which is set against a wide range of aperture settings so that once the film speed is set on to the meter the correct aperture is indicated, usually in increments of one-third of a stop. When taking incident light readings with a flash meter it is important to take into account that, unlike daylight photography, with studio flash it is quite likely that two or more light sources are being used and so you must ensure that only the main or key light registers on the meter. If, for example, a back-light or a rim light is being used and this is allowed to affect the meter it can result in an inaccurate reading.

Colour temperature meters

This is not an exposure meter but it works in a similar way. Its function is to determine the colour temperature of a light source in order to establish the filtration required to avoid a colour cast when the light source is incorrectly matched to the film in use. Colour transparency films are matched to a specific colour temperature – daylight film, for example, is designed to give a correct colour balance with a light source of 5,500° Kelvin and artificial light film for 3,200° Kelvin. There are, however, many situations in which the colour quality of the light source can fall outside these measurements – daylight can be as high as 10,000° Kelvin in open shade on a sunny day with a blue sky, for instance, or artificial light as low as 2,000° Kelvin, say from a candle. When the colour temperature is higher than that for which the film is balanced, the result will be a blue cast and a reddish filter must be used to correct it; when the colour temperature is lower, a reddish cast will be created and a bluish filter will be needed to produce a true colour balance. A colour temperature meter will give an accurate measurement of the colour temperature and will indicate the precise filtration required to balance it. However, its use is only necessary with transparency films in mixed or indeterminate lighting situations and for all but the most exacting work it is possible to estimate the filtration required.

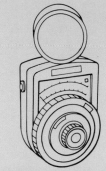

A colour temperature meter

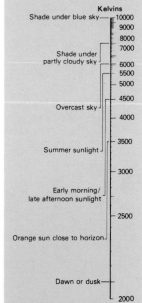

This diagram shows the range of colour temperatures in degrees Kelvin created by familiar light sources.

A colour temperature meter is only needed when shooting in indeterminate or mixed light for critical results.

FILTERS

Filters for Black-and-White Photography

As its name implies, a filter removes an element of the light which passes through it. The process is most easily understood if you think of white light being comprised of the three primary colours red, green and blue, each of which has a complementary colour which is a mixture of the other two hues. Thus the complementary colour of red is a mixture of green and blue which is cyan; the complementary of green is a mixture of red and blue called magenta; and the complementary of blue is a mixture of red and green which is yellow. Black-and-white film is equally sensitive to all three primary colours, and therefore of course to the complementary colours, so that a black-and-white shot of three coloured objects, red, green and blue, which are of equal brightness, will record on the film as the same tone of grey. If, however, a filter is introduced it will prevent the complementary colours passing through and they will not record on the film, thus creating a black tone instead of a grey on the print. In this way colour filters can be used in black-and-white photography to vary the tonal range and quality of a picture and to help define objects and also to alter the contrast of an image.

In practice, of course, objects are not usually of pure primary colours but rather of a mixture – a red flower, for instance, may reflect some blue and green light as well as red, so the effect of using a filter will not be so extreme, and also in normal cir-

The picture on the left, of blue flowers and green leaves in a red basket against a grey stone background, was taken without a filter and shows each colour as a similar tone of grey. The photograph on the right, however, shows the effect of using a blue filter making the basket and leaves darker.

cumstances the filters you use will seldom be of primary hues. The general rule to remember is that objects of a complementary colour to the filter in use will record as a darker tone on the print and objects of a similar colour will record as a lighter tone. A red flower in a blue vase against a green wall, for example, would, if photographed without a filter, record with each as equal tones of grey; with a red filter the blue vase and the green wall would appear much darker and the red flower would be lighter in tone; with a blue filter the red flower and the green wall would be substantially darker while the vase would be lighter in tone; and with a green filter the wall would appear lighter, with the flower and the vase much darker. The effect of the filter will depend on the actual colour of the object and the density of the filter in use.

It is also important to appreciate that the exposure will be affected since the filter is preventing some of the light from reaching the film; this can be calculated by using the filter factor which is supplied with each filter, one which has a factor of × 2 will require an increase of one stop, × 3 one and a half stops, and × 4 two stops extra, and so on. Another point when using TTL metering is that it is not always safe to assume that the reading given will adequately compensate for the filter since some cells used in exposure meters are not equally sensitive to all colours of light; it is therefore best to take the reading without the filter and alter the indicated exposure according to the filter factor.

The picture on the left shows the effect of using a green filter, making the red basket much darker in tone and the leaves lighter, while the photograph on the right was taken with a red filter, making the flowers and leaves much darker but the basket lighter in tone.

A filter-system kit

A gelatin filter holder with
a detachable lens hood

Filters are manufactured in a variety of forms: as glass discs mounted into a threaded metal ring which can be attached directly on to the camera lens, as plastic squares which can be slotted into a plastic frame which in turn fits on to the lens via a threaded adapter, or as thin acetate or gelatin squares which can either be taped over the lens or held in a special mount which fits on to the lens. Glass filters have the advantage of being of high optical quality and are also resistant to scratches and abrasions; their main disadvantage is that they are designed to fit a specific lens mount and if you have several lenses with different threads then you will need filters to fit each lens. One way round this is to buy a filter to fit the largest lens and to buy 'stepping' rings to convert the mount to fit the smaller lenses. The main advantage of the acetate or gelatin filters is that they are relatively inexpensive, thin enough to have a minimal effect on the definition of the lens and are made in a variety of colours including specialist uses such as tri-colour separation filters which are not obtainable in other forms, except at considerable expense. The disadvantage of the acetate filters is that as they are very vulnerable to damage and abrasion they cannot be cleaned, and therefore must be handled with considerable care in order to prolong their life. In recent years the plastic 'system' filters have become the most widely used type – they have the advantage of being relatively inexpensive, especially when larger-size filters are needed, they are of quite high optical quality and are relatively durable if handled with reasonable care. Their main advantage, however, is that they will fit a wide range of lens mounts since the filter holder can be fitted with a variety of threaded adapters for different lenses, and the mount will also hold several filters together.

Red filters

Red filters are useful for landscape photography since they can be used to reduce the effects of atmospheric haze, giving pictures with distant views greater clarity. They will also tend to make shadows stronger on a sunny day and will increase the contrast of an image. A deep red filter can also create dramatic effects when a blue sky is present particularly when there are white clouds, with the sky nearly black and the clouds shown in strong relief. A red filter is also very effective with black-and-white infra-red film, and will record green foliage as nearly white and blue sky as a very dark tone of grey. In portrait photography a red filter can be effective in improving the appearance of skin flaws, and red marks and spots will record much lighter in tone and will not be so noticeable; however, lips will also appear lighter in tone and this can appear unnatural particularly with a female subject, but this can be overcome by using a lipstick of a deeper and more bluish hue. Another use of a red filter is in accentuating the texture of wood and stone.

These two photographs show the effect of using a red filter. The unfiltered picture (*above*) has recorded the blue sky as quite a pale tone of grey with the clouds only barely discernible. The red filter used in the picture below, however, has recorded the sky as a much darker tone, showing the clouds in bold relief. An increase in exposure of 3 stops was needed to compensate for the filter.

A strong blue filter was used for this portrait to emphasize the rugged skin texture and to create richer tones. It needed 2 stops extra exposure.

Orange filters

An orange filter produces a similar though less extreme effect to that of a red filter. Its main use would be to make a blue sky a deeper tone in outdoor pictures, giving white clouds a more dramatic quality, but without the stark quality which a red filter would produce.

Yellow filters

These are used mainly for giving the appearance of blue skies and clouds a 'normal' quality in a photograph. Without a filter a blue sky tends to record too light in black-and-white pictures and the use of a yellow filter will create visually on the print the effect you see. A deep yellow filter is also useful if it is necessary to copy a black-and-white photograph or artwork which has become stained or discoloured.

A green filter was used to make the foliage in this landscape picture lighter and to create more contrast and texture. An increase in exposure of 2 stops was needed to compensate for the filter.

Green and blue filters

Filters of this type tend to be used less in black-and-white photography than those in the red to yellow range, but nevertheless there are some useful applications. A blue filter is effective in increasing the effects of haze or mist in landscape shots when this is desirable for atmosphere, for example. In this way it can also increase the impression of aerial perspective, the effect when progressively more distant planes in a picture become lighter in tone the closer

they are to the horizon. In portrait photography a blue filter is very useful for accentuating skin texture when the purpose of a picture is to reveal the character of the subject as opposed to flattery; it can be particularly effective when combined with low-key lighting. In landscape shots a blue filter can often help to create more contrast when there is a deep blue sky, since if this is unrelieved by clouds it can create a rather flat, grey quality; a blue filter will record it as a much lighter or white tone, helping to make details or objects against the skyline stand out more clearly. A green filter can also be of use in landscape photography as it will make green foliage a lighter tone and tend to increase both detail and contrast within it, particularly in the case of dense green summer foliage. The important thing to remember when selecting a filter is that it should be the same colour as the parts of the subject you want to make lighter in tone and the opposite or complementary colour to parts of the subject you want to record as a darker tone.

Graduated filters

Graduated filters are more widely used in colour photography, but they can be useful in black-and-white work. In these filters only half of the glass or plastic is tinted, with a gradual transition from tint to clear glass; this means that they can be used so that only part of the picture area is affected. Although they can be obtained as a circular glass design, the square filters are in fact more controllable as they can be moved laterally or horizontally within the filter mount so that the area affected by the filter can be adjusted precisely. The neutral-tone filter is very useful for reducing the brightness of a sky tone when shooting a landscape picture, for example; although with black-and-white pictures the sky can be made darker by printing in at the enlarging stage, if it is very over-exposed there will be a loss of detail and contrast that will be prevented by the use of a graduated filter. Similarly, there are occasions when an orange filter, for example, can be used to make a blue sky darker, but to avoid the effect of making any foreground foliage darker as well.

The neutral, graduated filter used to emphasize the dark, stormy sky in this photograph, has avoided the need for heavy printing-in at the enlargement stage.

Polarizing filters

In black-and-white photography a polarizing filter can be used to good effect in order to control reflections in non-metallic surfaces. When light is reflected from a shiny surface some of it is polarized, this means that instead of the light rays oscillating in all planes they do so only on one plane and are in effect parallel to each other like a grid. A polarizing filter has the same effect and when it is rotated so that the angle of oscillation is opposed to that of the light reflected from the surface it prevents it passing, and so the reflection itself, or at least that which has been polarized, is eliminated. This effect can be seen visually by looking through the filter at a reflective surface or object and rotating the filter. Since the filter is neutral grey in tone it has no effect on the tonal rendering of the colours within the subject except where this is affected by polarized light. For black-and-white shots this type of filter is probably most useful for shooting subjects that are under or behind glass, such as a picture for example or a shop window, and the reflections in the surface of water can also be eliminated or reduced. Since blue sky is created by the reflections from droplets of water in the atmosphere, this too can be affected by a polarizing filter; the effect will be dependent on the relative positions of the sun, camera and sky area being photographed, but at its maximum will give a darkening of tone similar to that of a deep yellow filter.

There are other uses of this type of filter – for example, to control reflections in objects such as polished wood, ceramics or glassware when taking still-life photographs. In portrait shots it can be helpful when photographing a model who wears glasses, for instance, and with landscape shots a polarizing filter can reduce the effects of atmospheric haze. Another less obvious use is to fit two filters to the lens to form a continuously variable neutral density filter to allow long exposures to be given, for example, or wide apertures to be used in

When the camera is loaded with fast film and you are photographing in very bright lighting conditions, a neutral density filter may be necessary to prevent overexposure.

bright light. By rotating one of the filters the amount of light passing through will be progressively reduced to the point where virtually no light is allowed through.

Neutral density filters

These filters are designed to reduce the amount of light passing through on to the film, and since they are grey in colour they have no effect on the tonal or colour quality of the image. They are available in a range of strengths, giving a reduction in brightness in increments of a third of a stop. There are a number of uses for these filters, to bring a particular subject brightness within the range of a camera, for example, if the camera is loaded with a fast film and is being used in bright sunlight. In this situation it is quite possible that even by selecting the fastest shutter speed and the smallest aperture the film will still be over-exposed, and this can be prevented by selecting a neutral density filter which will reduce the image brightness by the required amount. It is also sometimes necessary to give a long exposure in bright light in order to create an effect: the blurred quality of moving water, for example, can be very attractive when an exposure of several seconds is given, and a neutral density filter can be used to allow this exposure to be given. The use of very wide apertures to create selective focus effects is possible in bright lighting conditions with a neutral density filter when the subject brightness is beyond the range of the shutter speeds. These filters can also be used to control exposure with lenses which have a fixed aperture such as a mirror or catadioptric lens. A neural density filter can be a convenient and precise way of reducing the power of a flashgun when it is used for fill-in flash techniques, for example, by placing the filter over the flash tube, and for when you want to over- or under-expose for effect with automatic cameras that have a separate window for light readings, such as an instant picture camera. By placing a one-stop neutral density filter over the exposure sensor only, for example, you will obtain one stop extra exposure and by placing it over the camera lens only you will under-expose by one stop.

Filters for Colour Photography

The use of filters with colour film is quite different from its use with black-and-white materials: with the latter it is the tonal rendition of the subject that is important, whereas with the former it is the way colours are recorded on the film which is crucial. If the strongly coloured filters used for black-and-white pictures are used with colour film the result is simply to produce an over-all colour tint in the photograph, with other colours in the subject being lost or subdued. This can be used effectively on occasions to create a dramatic or unusual effect, but in normal practice filters of a much more subtle tint are used for colour shots.

UV or skylight filters

These are considered part of the basic kit by most photographers when shooting in colour. Although daylight colour film is manufactured to produce an image of correct colour balance when used in daylight, the range of colour temperature that can be created in outdoor lighting is very much wider than that for the precise colour temperature for which the film is balanced, and for most daylight films this is 5,500° Kelvin. The human eye is relatively insensitive to changes in the colour quality of the light and we tend to make adjustments quite subconsciously; in this way the difference between what we thought we saw and how it appears on the film can sometimes be quite considerable. One quite common situation in which the film is influenced by light waves that are invisible to the eye is in the case of ultra-violet light which will affect the blue sensitive layer of the film and create a corresponding blue cast in the photograph; where there is a strong presence of ultra-violet light this can be quite pronounced. This is common on cloudy or overcast days, at high altitudes and by the sea, and the use of an ultra-violet (UV) filter or a skylight filter is essential in these circumstances. Since these filters will have no adverse effect on the film when ultra-violet light is not present in a scene, many photographers prefer to leave them permanently in position on their lenses; an added advantage is that they offer some protection to the more costly lens, and if they are damaged they are relatively inexpensive to replace. It is important to bear in mind, however, that it is not advisable to use more filters than are strictly necessary since this can adversely affect the performance of the lens, and when an additional filter is being used and the UV filter is not necessary it is best to remove it. In addition to countering the potential blue cast, UV absorbing filters will also help to penetrate atmospheric haze, thus giving more clarity to pictures such as a distant view.

Colour balancing filters

Colour balancing filters are designed to correct an imbalance between the colour temperature of the light source and that for which the film is balanced, and since the colour temperature of daylight alone can vary enormously most photographers will find them essential. When the colour temperature is higher than that for which the film is balanced, the result will be a blue cast on the film and a yellowish filter will be needed to compensate. The most common situations in which this is likely to occur is on overcast or cloudy days and on sunny days with a blue sky when taking shots in open shade; however, since a blue cast is in most instances undesirable and in general a slightly warm or yellowish cast quite pleasing, it is usually preferable to use a warm filter in the 81 range if in any doubt. These are available in a range of strengths from 81A to 81D; the former is a fairly weak filter which just gives a slight degree of warmth to the image, and since it also absorbs UV light many photographers choose to leave them permanently in position on their lenses for most pictures in preference to the UV or skylight filter. The stronger filters, such as the 81B and the 81C, will have a more marked effect and should be used when the lighting conditions suggest that a positive blue cast might occur. Shooting in open shade on a day when there is a deep blue sky or shooting against the light when the subject is lit predominantly with reflected light are occasions when these filters are likely to be needed; this is particularly true when taking portraits since skin

A Wratten 81B filter was used for this portrait taken indoors using daylight from a north facing window – conditions which can often create a cold image. The additional warmth, which was created by the filter, gives a more pleasing effect.

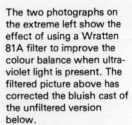

The two photographs on the extreme left show the effect of using a Wratten 81A filter to improve the colour balance when ultra-violet light is present. The filtered picture above has corrected the bluish cast of the unfiltered version below.

This abstract nude picture was taken in the studio using electronic flash and a Wratten 81B to create a warmer and more flattering skin quality.

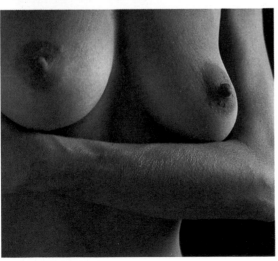

tones are especially sensitive to colour casts and a bluish cast in a portrait can be quite unpleasant. In these circumstances it can even help to over-compensate deliberately to create additional warmth in the picture, and this is also true of nude and glamour pictures where it is vital for the model's skin to look as appealing as possible.

Shooting with daylight indoors is another situation in which a warm filter is likely to be needed since the light is usually indirect and reflected from the sky. A warm filter can also improve the colour quality of a picture when direct flash is used, as this often creates a colder or more bluish image than when it is diffused or reflected. An 81A or 81B filter is helpful when a polarizing filter is being used since this will tend to emphasize the blue tones in a picture, such as sea and sky, and the same can apply to the use of long telephoto lenses where the bluish quality of haze can influence the colour quality of a picture which concentrates the attention on the more distant aspects of a scene. The colour temperature of daylight becomes lower than that for which the film is balanced when the sun is lower in the sky, and in general the warmer, mellower light of early morning or late afternoon is a desirable quality, and it would not usually be considered necessary to use a bluish colour balancing filter to correct it; however, where it is necessary to do so, with a portrait, for example, or when it is important to record the colours of a subject accurately, then filters in the 82 range should be used. These filters are more likely to be needed in artificial light conditions when non-standard photographic lighting is being used. Ordinary domestic lighting, for example, has a substantially lower colour temperature than that for which tungsten light film is balanced, and if filters are not used a pronounced reddish or warm cast will be created. It should be remembered, however, that it is not only the colour temperature of the light source that affects the colour quality of a picture. The colour of the surroundings can also have an influence: light reflected from brightly coloured walls, for example, when shooting indoors could create a colour cast and this should also be allowed for when selecting a filter.

The colour balancing filters mentioned so far are for relatively minor differences in colour temperature, but much stronger filters are also available when the light source is quite different from that for which the film is balanced. It is possible, for instance, to shoot daylight film in tungsten light by using an 80A or an 80B filter, and artificial light film can be used in daylight or with electronic flash with the aid of an 85 or 85B filter. Shooting colour film under fluorescent light is rather less straightforward since the colour temperature and composition of fluorescent tubes are quite variable. Some filter manufacturers supply a fluorescent conversion filter for use with daylight film but this is rather a compromise and will not by any means give a correctly balanced picture with every tube and it is best to use the colour compensating filters such as the Kodak Wratten gelatin filters. As a general rule, using daylight film with daylight-type tubes will require filtration in the order of CC30 Magenta and this can be used as the basis for a test.

Colour compensating filters

These are available in gelatin squares in a range of both primary and complementary colours in different strengths, and they can be mixed to give a wide range of correction – for example, with a warm white tube photographed on daylight type Ektachrome 200 film Kodak recommend the use of a CC40 Cyan and a CC40 Magenta filter. These filters are also ideal for making the small corrections sometimes needed for a particular batch of film when critical results are required or when long exposures are given, creating reciprocity failure, which often produces a colour cast. Colour compensating filters need of course not only be used for correcting a colour cast, and the creative photographer will find them equally useful for introducing or emphasizing a colour cast in order to create effects or to add atmosphere to a picture. The range also includes specialist filters for use with materials such as infra-red film – the Kodak Wratten 12 filter can create dramatic and unusual effects with Infra-Red Ektachrome film, recording green foliage as red or magenta tones. Unusual effects can also be

A tobacco-coloured filter was used for this seascape, both to make the sky darker and to add colour, giving the impression of a sunset.

This abstract photograph of reflections in rippled water was taken with the aid of an orange filter normally used for black-and-white photography. In this instance it has added impact and interest to what was essentially a colourless subject.

The landscape picture (*far left*) was taken using a polarizing filter. Although it was a very cloudly and overcast day, the filter has enabled quite rich and saturated colours to be recorded.

produced by using colour filters in combination
with multiple exposures – tri-colour separation
filters, for example, can be used to make three
separate exposures on to the same piece of film so
that the static elements of a scene are recorded in
natural colour but moving elements such as water
will have a multi-coloured appearance.

Polarizing filters

In addition to their usefulness in controlling the
tones of an image through their effect on reflected
light, polarizing filters are also extremely effective
in influencing the colour quality of an image. Since
it is a neutral grey in appearance, a polarizing filter
will not affect the over-all colour quality of a
picture, but it will alter the appearance of coloured
surfaces that reflect light. The best example of this
is a blue sky which is created by light reflected from
droplets of water in the atmosphere; by eliminating
some of this reflected, polarized light the sky not
only becomes darker in tone but also a richer and
stronger colour. A similar effect is also created with
water and a polarizing filter can have a quite
dramatic effect with seascapes on a sunny day.
However, even on a cloudy day it can still be effective, as many objects and surfaces in outdoor situations are quite reflective and will benefit from the
use of a polarizing filter; green summer foliage in a
landscape shot, for instance, will be recorded with
greater depth of colour, and distant views will often
have more definition and clarity when some of the
reflected light is eliminated with a polarizing filter.
A polarizing filter can be useful in making tanned
skin a richer and deeper colour, especially when
combined with a Wratten 81B. This technique is
often used in nude and glamour photography.

Graduated filters

Graduated filters are particularly useful in colour
photography as they enable selective areas of a
picture to be altered tonally or for the colour to be
changed. When shooting black-and-white or colour
negative film it is possible to make certain areas of
the print darker or lighter by shading or printing-in
when the enlargement is made, and the graduated

filter makes this effect possible with a colour transparency. Possibly the most useful aspect of this is in landscape photography when a graduated filter can be used to make the sky a darker tone. The exposure needed for foreground details often means that the sky is over-exposed, resulting in a lack of tone and colour, and a graduated filter can be used to prevent this, as the neutral or grey filter will have no effect on the colour of the sky. There are, however, a wide range of coloured versions that can be used to introduce colour into an area, and in this way the impression of a sunset can be created artificially, but it is easy to overdo this and produce rather gimmicky pictures. As a general rule, the coloured filters are more effective when they are used to reinforce or emphasize a colour which already exists: sometimes the colour created in a sunset can be a little disappointing and the use of an appropriate graduated filter such as a tobacco or a mauve can add more colour and drama to the shot. It is not only sky areas, however, that can benefit from these filters, and they can also be used to make other parts of the picture darker or to prevent it from over-exposing: a foreground of back-lit water, for example, where the highlights are too strong could be controlled in this way. In some situations a graduated filter can be used to balance the difference in brightness between interior and exterior details and can also help to prevent the foreground over-exposing when flash is used. It should be remembered, however, that since the purpose of a graduated filter is to make part of the picture darker you must when using TTL metering take the exposure readings *before* the filter is fitted otherwise its effect will be negated.

In addition to graduated filters *Centre Spot* filters are also available, using a similar principle; these can be used to make the outside of a picture darker and with a colour cast leaving the central area unaffected. However, they do produce a much more obvious and 'tricky' effect and must be used sparingly to avoid over-gimmicky pictures. Two inverted, graduated filters of different tints can also be used to create colour changes in both the foreground and distant details of a picture.

Effects Filters and Attachments

A colourburst filter has been used to create the rainbow streaks in this close-up picture taken into the light.

There are a variety of filters and glass or plastic attachments designed to produce a range of effects that can be obtained as individual accessories or as part of a filter system such as the Cokin. Used with the right subject and with a little discretion most of these can be used to contribute to the effect of a picture – however, this proviso is important since the idea is often promoted that the effects themselves can create a worthwhile picture, and this is in fact not so.

A soft-focus attachment has created a more romantic quality in this landscape shot.

The use of a soft-focus attachment in this portrait has created a more flattering and pleasing skin quality.

Soft-focus or diffusion filters

Most modern camera lenses are capable of recording the finest detail with pin-sharp accuracy and for most pictures this is what is wanted, yet there are occasions when a softer, less defined image is more effective. The principle of these attachments is that finely engraved or moulded lines in the filter create a degree of interference as the light rays pass through the lens and prevent it from recording fine detail; filters with varying degrees of diffusion are available but even the strongest effect is quite different from that produced by the image being simply out of focus, since with a soft-focus attachment there is an underlying core of sharpness which holds the image together. The effect of these filters can be judged visually on the screen when using an SLR or view camera but with a viewfinder camera this is not possible.

One of the most useful applications of this type of filter is in portrait or nude photography where skin is often more appealing when its texture and also of course any blemishes are subdued or masked by soft-focus techniques. In addition to producing less definition these attachments tend to reduce the contrast of the image, and this can also be a desirable effect when shooting this type of subject in colour, as it creates a more flattering and less harsh quality. These effects can combine to create pictures with a gentler, more romantic mood, especially when applied to subjects with harmonious or pastel colours. David Hamilton is a photographer of the nude who has developed a personal style by means of this quality and his work is a perfect example of how the essential realism of a photograph can be subdued to heighten the impression of fantasy and romanticism.

Lighting is also affected by soft-focus attachments, and subjects that contain bright highlights, such as a back-lit shot for example, will take on an almost luminous glow and this can be just as effective with landscapes and still-life shots as it is with portraits and nudes. In addition, soft focus can contribute to the effect of grainy photographs – pictures taken on fast, coarse-grained film like 3M's ISO 1000/31 and enlarged to a considerable degree will show the grain even more when the fine details of the subject are reduced by diffusion.

Pastel or fog filters

Pastel or fog filters are also very useful in helping to control the quality of the image; they have a slightly milky appearance and their effect is to reduce the contrast of a picture quite drastically. They are available in two strengths and also in a graduated version which means that they can be used to create the effect of distant haze or fog while leaving the foreground of the picture with normal contrast and clarity. As well as reducing the contrast they also reduce the colour saturation with colour photographs, and when used with a degree of over-exposure can create quite soft pastel colours from even a brightly coloured subject, giving a quality similar to that of a soft-focus attachment but much stronger and with less effect on the definition of the picture. In addition to being used to create an effect for its own sake, they can be used to reduce the contrast of an image that would otherwise be too great for the film to record, and similarly in some circumstances when making colour prints or duplicate transparencies from a contrasty original slide.

Starburst filters

These are filters which create streaks of light radiating from highlights or light sources within the picture area. They are available in a variety of configurations ranging from just four streaks to sixteen. They can be equally effective with both black-and-white and colour shots but the best results will be obtained when the background of the shot is quite dark in tone. These attachments will also reduce contrast, and in some circumstances it can be beneficial to make a double exposure, one without the filter to record the scene itself and another giving two or three stops less with the starburst attachment to record the streaks of light. The effect of the filter will be dependent on both the focal length of the lens and the aperture used: with a wide-angle lens and a small aperture the streaks will be smaller and more defined than with a wide aperture or a longer focal length lens.

These two pictures show the effect of using a pastel or fog filter. The filtered version on the left has much softer colours and lower contrast than one on the right.

A starburst filter has been used to create the radiating streaks of light from the sun in this landscape shot.

Colourburst filters

Colourburst filters (or diffraction gratings) have a similar effect to that of the starburst filter, except that they create coloured streaks of light from highlights and light sources. Consequently, they are only suitable for colour photography and are also more effective when the subject has an essentially dark background. There is a wide selection of configurations, ranging from something similar to the radiating streaks of the starburst to those which create horizontal or circular bands of colour. Unlike the starburst, however, these attachments can create interesting effects when only moderate highlights or areas of light are present in the picture area.

Prismatic attachments

These are used to create repeated images of a central subject. They are available in a variety of configurations, some creating additional images around the central subject and others producing a lateral repetition. The choice of lens and aperture will also influence the effect created – a wide-angle lens will create a more separated and defined series of images, whereas a long-focus lens will tend to produce a more subtle merging effect, as will the choice of a wide aperture. This type of attachment is most effective when used with a subject that is well separated from the background and has a bold and well-defined shape, like a silhouetted tree for example, and with colour shots it will produce a more dramatic effect if there is a strong colour contrast between subject and background. It is also possible to buy a single prism attachment which, when placed in front of the lens and angled correctly, will produce a very soft-focus, rainbow-fringed image of the subject.

Filter masks

These attachments are designed either for producing a black vignetted frame around the picture or to enable double exposures to be combined in the same shot. The first simply provides a variety of cut-out shapes such as an oval or binocular aperture to place over the lens; the choice of aperture and focal length of lens will determine how well defined the frame appears in the photograph. Double exposure masks are designed so that one exposure is made with a mask preventing part of the film being exposed, and the second exposure is then made through the other mask which shields the area of film which has already been exposed, allowing the two images to be blended together. In this way it is possible to photograph the same person twice against the same background, but it is of course vital to use a tripod since the camera must not be moved between the two exposures.

Split-field attachments

A split-field attachment is used to enable both very close and distant objects to be recorded sharply. It is in effect half a close-up lens, and when placed over the lower half of the camera lens allows it to focus at a much closer distance, while not affecting the focus at the top of the picture, thus giving the impression of very great depth of field. It is important to ensure, however, that it is positioned so that the edge of the filter coincides with an area of the subject that has little or no detail otherwise its presence will be quite noticeable.

Colour-back filters

These attachments, which are used to create effects with flash photographs, consist simply of a matched pair of complementary filters so that, when combined, they cancel each other out – like red and cyan for example. The principle is that, when combining flash and ambient light, one filter is placed over the camera lens, the red for example, which will create a red cast over the whole of the image, but if the cyan filter is then placed over the flash the foreground which is illuminated will be brought back to the correct colour balance, leaving the more distant areas with the red cast because they are unaffected by the flash. The same pair of filters can of course be reversed so that the background can be given a blue cast. The effect will be more dramatic when the background has an obviously distorted colour, like making the sky appear green for instance, and can be further emphasized by under-exposing the exposure for the ambient light by one or two stops.

WORKING AIDS

Camera Cases
Camera Maintenance
Stands and Tripods

Camera Cases

Photographic equipment is both expensive and fragile and therefore requires careful handling and storage in order to keep it in good working order. The first, and probably the most important, aspect of camera care is to have a good camera bag. There are two main choices: the hard, suitcase-style case with either plastic foam inserts or dividers, and the soft case with padded compartments. The former offers the greatest protection to the equipment and is certainly the best choice if you will be travelling when it will be necessary for your equipment to be handled by other people, at airports for example.

An adjustable rigid case

The plastic foam can be cut to fit the equipment exactly and if generous space is left around each item it can survive quite careless handling very well. The problem with this system, of course, is that the case is then designed for specific equipment and cannot easily accommodate extra or different items. This same type of case can also be obtained with movable dividers, but they do not offer the same degree of protection against damage by impact. The main disadvantage of the rigid case is that it is not very convenient or comfortable for carrying and using from the shoulder. Another point is that it is very obviously identifiable as a camera case which can invite interest from thieves and also makes it difficult to avoid attracting attention when shooting in situations where you want to keep a low profile.

A rigid equipment case

The soft camera bags overcome these problems but are not really suitable for situations where they might be dropped or banged, such as in the luggage hold of a plane for instance, but on the other hand they can easily be stowed under an aircraft seat or on the overhead rack. Many experienced photographers like to use two cases when they are travelling – the rigid suitcase type for transporting the equipment and a soft fabric case to which individual items can be transferred as and when required for actual use.

A soft-fabric case

Special cases are also available for the more active photographer, such as waist and back packs for walking or climbing and waterproof buoyancy cases

A belt with pouches

for use in marine photography. It is also possible to buy jackets specially made for the photographer with pouches and compartments built into the garment to hold items of equipment, which means that a complete camera outfit can be 'worn' without the need for separate bags and cases. As a general rule, individual items can be kept in the cases supplied for the purpose by the manufacturer, such as the ever-ready cases for cameras and hard cases or soft pouches for lenses for example, but while it is a good idea to store equipment in these cases when not in use, a compartment case will be much more practical and provide better access when a number of items are to be carried around together. A well-organized case can make all the difference.

A waistcoat with built-in compartments and pouches for equipment

Camera Maintenance

Camera maintenance should be restricted only to cleaning the equipment and anything more than this left to a reliable camera mechanic. At the same time, however, it is vital to ensure that all equipment is kept free of dust and moisture and that lenses and other glass surfaces are not allowed to become smeary. There are a number of accessories that are helpful in this respect. A blower brush or aerosol air spray can be used to remove surface dust and grit from both interior and exterior surfaces, and this should be done before any other cleaning is carried out. A selvyt cloth or lens cleaning tissues are the correct materials for gentle wiping of glass surfaces; for obstinate smears a little lens cleaning fluid can be used sparingly, but remember that the less it is necessary to handle lenses the better, and that the least possible pressure should be applied. In addition to the routine cleaning of your camera, it is also advisable to check periodically that all the controls and functions are operating correctly. Open up the camera back, for example, when it is empty and fire the shutter a few times to check that the blinds or leaves are moving as they should and that the iris mechanism is closing down properly to the selected aperture. Remember too to check the flash synchronization occasionally by firing it whilst looking through the camera back.

A blower brush for the removal of dust and grit from lenses and other delicate surfaces

An air-spray can for gentle cleaning of glass surfaces

Stands and Tripods

A camera stand or a heavy tripod is a vital accessory for studio work, particularly when large-format cameras are used. They are also essential for still-life subjects like this flower arrangement opposite.

One of the most important factors in producing sharp pictures is the avoidance of camera shake. Using fast shutter speeds will do much to accomplish this when using a hand-held camera but even this is not the complete answer if the camera is not securely supported. There are, however, a wide range of accessories available to help overcome this problem. Supports to aid hand-held shooting include monopods, rifle grips and hand brackets, and all of them can be used to reduce the risk of camera shake when using slower shutter speeds or when using long-focus lenses when the risk of camera shake is much greater.

The best solution to this problem is undoubtedly a camera stand, and few accessories can improve the results of even a simple camera so effectively. A stand is essential for large-format view cameras, and for studio work many photographers prefer the centre column stand to the conventional tripod; this has the advantage of extreme rigidity and swift and positive adjustment, being able to move a camera in seconds from just above floor level to a height of about 3 metres (10 feet). The camera is held on an adjustable horizontal arm which allows it to be aimed straight down for overhead still-life shots or copying. The obvious disadvantage of this type of stand is that it is simply not portable and for location work a tripod is necessary. When choosing a tripod, the best advice is to make sure it is as rigid and solid as the weight you are prepared to carry will permit. A centre column will give you a degree of quick vertical adjustment, and braced legs will prevent the tripod legs slipping apart on some surfaces; with an eye-level camera like an SLR it can be much more convenient to choose a tripod that will support the camera at a height which will avoid the need for you to stoop constantly. The lever type of leg locks can be quicker to use than the twist rings and are perhaps less vulnerable to jamming. The tripod head is also an important consideration: a ball and socket head allows quick adjustment and can be easier to use with a camera like a 35 mm where it needs to be frequently changed from a

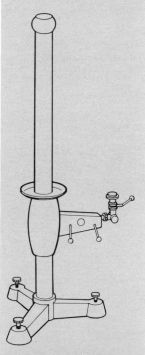

A heavyweight, wheel-based column, camera stand for studio use and for large-format cameras

For subjects where maximum depth of field is important, like in this landscape shot, a tripod will allow a small aperture and a correspondingly slow shutter speed to be used without the risk of camera shake.

A tripod or camera stand is very useful for portrait photography as it allows the camera to be precisely aimed and focused and then left in position whilst other adjustments, to lighting and so on, are made.

horizontal to a vertical position, but at the same time the pan and tilt head offers more precise control since it can be adjusted separately for vertical and horizontal alignment.

Many people do not fully appreciate the advantages of using a tripod – they can be far more useful than for just avoiding the risk of camera shake, and can improve the quality of pictures in other ways as well as adding to the scope of a camera. Using a tripod will enable you to frame your pictures much more precisely, particularly with subjects close to the camera such as a portrait, and when working in a studio or with lighting equipment you will be able to leave your camera in position on a tripod while you make adjustments to the lighting and background, for example. In addition, a tripod will allow you to devote more attention to your model and to communicate more directly with him or her rather than through the camera's viewfinder. Because a tripod will allow you to use slower shutter speeds without the risk of camera shake you will also be able to use smaller apertures, which will in turn give you greater depth of field; this can be particularly important with subjects close to the camera, such as close-up shots or still-life pictures, or even with a landscape shot when sharp detail is needed in both close and distant objects. Without a tripod you are rarely able to use the shutter speeds on a camera slower than about 1/30 sec, whereas with the camera firmly supported there is virtually

A portable tripod

A ball and socket head for a tripod or camera stand

A pan and tilt head for a tripod

This sunset picture, taken long after the sun had gone down, needed an exposure of several seconds, making the use of a tripod vital. The film was rated at half its indicated speed to allow for reciprocity failure.

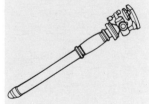

A monopod with an adjustable head

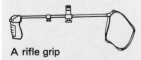

A rifle grip

no limit to the length of the exposure you can give, and this can dramatically increase the range of both the subjects and the conditions in which you shoot.

Low light conditions in outdoor photography often produce the most interesting and attractive pictures – after the sun has gone down, for example, or with street lights at night – and this type of subject is possible even with a simple camera when it is mounted on a tripod. Giving long exposures is often the most satisfactory way of photographing large interiors such as a church which would be very difficult to light artificially, and providing the picture is framed to avoid including extremes of contrast and light sources like large areas of window, existing light can be used very effectively. It is important to appreciate, however, that with very long exposures you can experience problems with what is known as reciprocity failure. In normal circumstances with exposures from, say, half a

second to a 1/1000 sec if you double the exposure the image will respond in the same way as if you opened the aperture by one stop, and it would become one stop lighter, however with very long exposures of a second or more this no longer happens, and doubling the exposure will have less effect on the film, and in effect its ISO rating becomes lower. The amount by which this varies depends on the type of film and the length of the exposure, and it is best to experiment with the film you generally use. As a guide, you can halve the ISO rating with exposures from one to 10 seconds, divide it by a third with exposures from 10 to 20 seconds, and rate the film at a quarter of its stated ISO rating with exposures from 20 to 40 seconds. Some layers in the emulsion of colour films are more affected by this than others and this can also produce a colour cast with long exposures, so it is advisable to anticipate this by making test exposures.

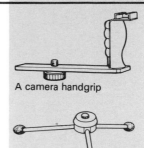

A camera handgrip

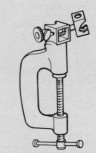

A table-top tripod for still-life and close-up pictures

A tripod was used for this close-up picture. This eliminates the risk of camera shake and allows a small aperture to be used to obtain sufficient depth of field.

A camera clamp with a ball and socket head

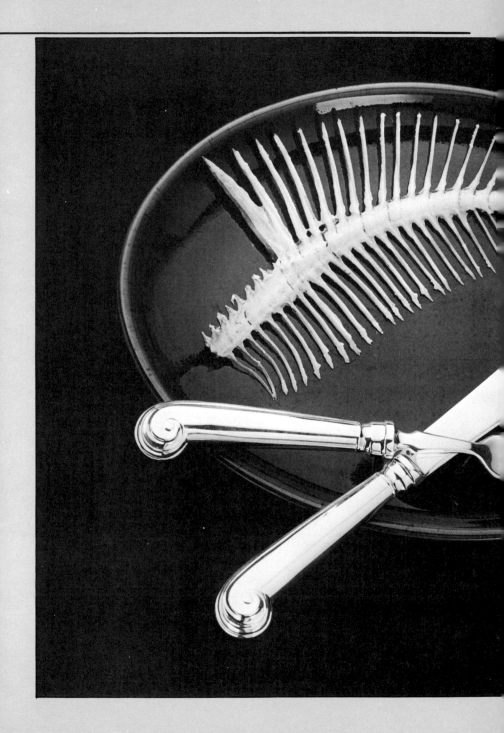

LIGHTING EQUIPMENT

Flash-Guns

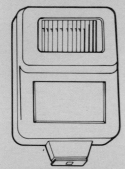

A simple flash-gun for which the guide-number method must be used for exposure calculation

A flash-gun is almost an obligatory accessory for most photographers, indeed many cameras are now made with a built-in flash-gun, and if used with a little thought and care a flash-gun can do much to increase the scope of your photography. On the other hand, however, poor flash pictures are probably one of the most common reasons for disappointing results. There are a number of different types of flash-gun and each has its own advantages and uses. The most basic type is battery-powered and fits directly into the accessory shoe of the camera. The exposure is determined by the use of a guide number, and the correct aperture is calculated by dividing the distance between the flash-gun and the subject into the guide number supplied for the film speed being used – for example, a gun with a guide number of 80 (in feet) for a film of ISO 100/21 when used 10 feet from the subject would need an aperture of f8. A more sophisticated form of exposure calculation uses a sensor in the flash-gun to measure the light reflected from the subject and automatically cuts off when it has received the correct exposure according to the film speed set and the aperture selected. This works in a similar way to an averaging exposure meter so it can be misled by a subject that has an unusual tonal range or is predominantly light or dark in nature, such as a bride in a white dress. In the case of many cameras with TTL metering there is a special dedicated flash-gun available which utilizes the camera's own exposure metering system to regulate the flash so it will still give an accurate result if the light from the flash is reflected from a wall or a ceiling, for example.

Another feature which varies between different types of flash-gun is output; the small, inexpensive flash-guns and those that are built in can provide enough light for subjects which are quite close to the camera and when the gun is aimed directly at the subject, but are inadequate for more distant subjects or for bouncing the light from a ceiling, for example, unless a very fast film is used. It is also important to consider the recycling time, as low-power, inexpensive flash-guns can take a consider-

Bouncing the light from a flash-gun off a white wall or ceiling creates a softer and more even light and a more natural effect than direct flash.

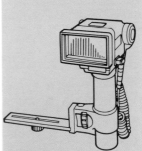

A more powerful hammer-head flash-gun with the facility to swivel and angle the head for bounce-flash techniques

able time to recharge in readiness for the next exposure, making it impossible to take shots in quick succession. With the more powerful flash-guns there is the added advantage that nickel cadmium rechargeable cells are available as an alternative to batteries, and these can make recycling even faster so that it is possible, for example, to take flash pictures when using a motor drive.

Although it is quite convenient to fix and connect the gun to the camera by means of a hot shoe, there are many occasions when it is best to hold the flash above or to one side of the camea, and for this reason it can be preferable to choose a gun that can also be connected to the camera with a conventional synchronizing lead. When using bounce or reflected flash it can be an advantage to have a flash-gun which has a head that can be swivelled, ideally both laterally and vertically. Some flash-guns with this facility also have a second flash-tube which remains aimed directly at the subject to alleviate the excessive top-light effect that can result with bounce flash. Many of the more advanced guns can be fitted with attachments which spread the light over a wider

A flash-gun with automatic exposure control governed by a separate light sensor

field, allowing it to be used with a wide-angle lens, or to concentrate the light for use over a greater distance when using a long-focus lens.

Whatever the choice of flash-gun, there are a few basic techniques which can greatly improve the quality of the pictures you take. It is important to bear in mind that the light from a flash-gun decreases in intensity in proportion to the square of the distance it is from the subject, so that at 3 metres (10 feet), for example, the light is only one-quarter of the brightness it is at 1.5 metres (5 feet); this means that when the exposure is calculated for a subject 1.5 metres away, objects 3 metres away will be two stops under-exposed. This causes one of the most common faults of flash photographs where objects (often people) close to the camera are seen against a black void. The solution is to ensure that your subject is quite close to the background, particularly if it is dark in tone, and similarly to avoid objects much closer to the camera than the subject for which the exposure is calculated as these will be considerably over-exposed and bleached out. When the flash is attached to the camera the light is very flat, and it can sometimes be possible to improve the effect of the lighting by holding the flash-gun slightly above and to one side of the camera; this will create more modelling in the subject and is often more satisfactory than flash on camera particularly when taking a portrait. It will also avoid the risk of 'red eye' which is caused when the flash-gun

More modelling sense can be created by holding the flash above and to one side of the camera position; a useful technique for portraits and one which avoids a shadow being cast onto the background.

is too close to the camera lens, causing the light to be reflected from the back of the subject's retina.

When taking pictures in a fairly small interior such as a domestic room it can also be more effective to aim the flash at a wall or ceiling rather than directly at the subject; in this way its light is reflected and diffused before it reaches the subject and creates a softer, more even light, often giving a more flattering and pleasing effect. It is important that the surface at which the flash-gun is aimed is light in tone, and when shooting in colour it must also be neutral in colour; ceilings are often the best choice since they are usually white. Obviously the exposure is affected by this technique as not only does the light have to travel further to reach the subject but it is also dispersed by the reflective surface. When using a dedicated flash this will be taken into account by the camera's metering system, and automatic flash-guns that enable the flash-head to be tilted while the sensor remains aimed at the subject will also give a corrected exposure; with other flash-guns, however, the exposure has to be calculated and this can be done by using the distance from the gun to the reflecting surface and from there to the subject to calculate the aperture, using the guide number, and then to open up one stop more to allow for the extra dispersion of the light. One danger to be avoided when using this technique with a ceiling is to ensure that you are not too close to your subject as this will create an excessively top light with unflattering shadows under the eyes and chin; this is where a flash-gun with a second tube which remains aimed directly at the subject can be an advantage.

Another technique which can often improve the quality of pictures taken with a single flash-gun is to use a longer exposure than that normally selected for the flash setting. This is usually between about 1/60 sec and 1/125 sec, and when taking pictures in low-light levels this will not be long enough to record the ambient light with the relatively small apertures usually used for flash exposures. However, by setting your shutter to a slower speed such as 1/30 sec or even less you will be able to record some of the existing light as well as that pro-

A flash-gun with a wide-angle adapter to spread the light over a wider field of view

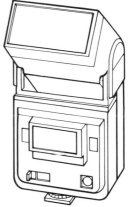

A flash-gun with a second flash tube which provides frontal fill-in light when the main head is used to bounce the light from a white wall or ceiling

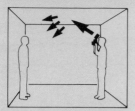

This diagram shows how a flash-gun can be used to bounce the light from a white ceiling to diffuse it.

vided by the flash. Be careful to avoid camera shake since this can create a ghost image where the area lit by the flash and the parts of the subject lit by ambient light meet, and when using shutter speeds slower than 1/30 sec it is advisable to use a tripod or some other support.

In addition to using a flash-gun as the sole source of light it can also be used to supplement existing light; this can be particularly effective in outdoor pictures in sunlight, for example, where the contrast is too great for the film to record satisfactorily, such as when the subject is strongly side-lit or when shooting into the light. To calculate the exposure in these circumstances it is easiest to consider the daylight and flash exposures separately. First take a normal daylight exposure reading that will record the lighter parts of the subject correctly leaving the shadows too dense – assume this is 1/125 at f8, for example – then calculate the exposure for the flash exposure in the normal way, dividing its distance from the subject into the guide number, also f8, for example. Since the flash is only being used in effect to 'fill in' or illuminate the shadows, it is not desirable to give the full flash exposure as this will create an artificial effect by eliminating the shadows completely; it is therefore necessary to under-expose the flash by about two stops so the aperture setting must be changed to f16, and to maintain the correct exposure for the daylight element of the picture the shutter speed must be re-set to 1/30 sec to compensate for the smaller aperture.

Flash can also be used in a similar way to create the impression of sunlight on a dull day by simply reversing the balance of exposure. In this case you must give the full flash exposure but under-expose the daylight by two stops; it is also necessary to position the flash-gun so that the angle of the shadows it casts are compatible with that which sunlight would create. A flash-gun can also be used to create dramatic lighting effects in combination with daylight – for example to create the effect of a night shot in broad daylight – for this technique the areas of the subject which are lit predominantly by daylight must be considerably under-exposed by as much as three or four stops with the full exposure given for the flash. This can be particularly effective when the subject is silhouetted against a moody sky, for example; in this type of situation it is often necessary to use quite fast shutter speeds to create the necessary degree of under-exposure, and when using a camera with a focal plane shutter such as a 35 mm SLR this may be limited to about 1/125 sec to ensure proper synchronization. In this case it can be overcome by removing the flash-gun from the camera and placing it much closer to the subject using a long flash lead to allow a smaller aperture to be used to reduce the daylight exposure.

Another very effective use of flash is to illuminate close-up subjects; this has the advantage that small apertures can be used for extra depth of field and at the same time the risk of camera shake or subject movement is reduced. One problem with this, however, can be that the camera itself can limit the angle and direction of the light because it is close to the subject; if the flash is placed too far to one side it will create an excessively contrasty and directional light, and this can be overcome to some extent by using a white reflector on the opposite side to reflect light back into the shadows. Another method is to place a piece of optical glass in front of the camera lens at an angle of 45° and to position the flash-gun at right-angles to the camera aimed at the angled surface of the glass; this will reflect the flash light along the optical path of the camera lens towards the subject but will not affect the camera's view.

It can often be more effective to select a slower shutter speed than that of the normal flash setting as this will enable the ambient light to record as well as the flash, like the light from the fire in this picture.

Accessories

Ring flash

A ring flash for close-up photography

Ring flash is an accessory designed especially for close-up photography. It is in effect a circular flash-tube which fits around the lens mount, enabling it not only to provide a direct, unobscured light to the subject but also to create a soft, even and shadowless illumination ideal for revealing detail in close-up subjects such as medical and dental work. There are a variety of different models, ranging from a simple flash-tube to ones with a series of tubes ranged within a circular reflector which fits around the lens. This latter type allows one or more of the tubes to be switched off so that as well as creating an even, shadowless light it is also possible to make it more directional; these accessories usually have a separate power pack. Ring flash can also be used to interesting effect when used at some distance from the subject: in addition to creating a flat frontal light which can be quite flattering it also produces an interesting rim of shadow around the subject.

A ring flash was used for this close-up shot to provide a direct but shadowless light source for maximum detail.

Slave cells

The possibilities of flash lighting can be considerably increased by the use of more than one gun. In this way a second source can be used to create rim-lighting or to illuminate the background, for example, independently of the subject lighting. The additional flash-guns can be fired simultaneously by the use of a slave cell, a light-sensitive device which fits into the sync lead socket of the flash-gun; when it 'receives' the light from the flash triggered by the camera it responds instantly. Slave cells are sensitive enough to be used at some distance from the main gun and can also work when not in direct view of the flash.

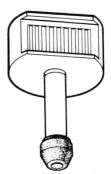

A slave cell for triggering multiple flash arrangements

A single flash-gun can also be used to illuminate quite large areas such as an interior when the subject is static and the camera is mounted on a tripod. The procedure is to set the camera on a time exposure and to fire the flash by hand, illuminating a small section of the subject in turn. The exposure can be calculated by setting the correct aperture for the flash-to-subject distance for each section, keeping this as constant as possible for each flash. It is necessary to ensure that the aperture selected and the length of time the shutter is open are such that any ambient light will not have an adverse effect on the over-all lighting.

A second flash-gun triggered by a slave cell was used to illuminate the background in this portrait, creating a more dramatic and interesting effect.

Lighting Equipment

While a small flash-gun can be used quite effectively in many circumstances it does of course have limitations, and a photographer who intends to use lighting for subjects where fine control and adjustment are needed, such as portrait or still-life work, will need to consider more elaborate equipment. The main limitations of the small flash-guns are lack of power and the inability to judge the effect of the lighting visually.

Photolamps

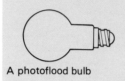

A photoflood bulb

These are the least expensive means of artificial lighting. They are similar to ordinary domestic bulbs but are more powerful; this is achieved by 'over-running', giving a higher output in exchange for a shorter life of only a few hours. They have the advantage of being relatively inexpensive and can be fitted into conventional bulb holders.

Tungsten halogen bulbs

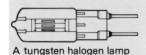

A tungsten halogen lamp

Tungsten halogen lighting uses a much smaller round or tube-shaped bulb without a filament which gives a more efficient and powerful illumination than photolamps. They also give a more constant output throughout their life. The disadvantage of this type of lighting is that the bulbs are more expensive and, being relatively fragile, have to be handled with some care, and must be used in special holders and reflectors.

Studio flash units

These provide the third option for artificial lighting and are available in a range of power and types. Unlike small flash-guns, these units are mostly powered by the mains supply although some systems can be adapted for use with batteries. They are provided with a continuous tungsten or halogen light as well as a flash-tube so the exact effect of the lighting can be seen, with the flash providing the light for the exposure. The least expensive and powerful type is the monobloc design in which the flash-head and power pack are incorporated into a single unit, making it quite compact and portable and easy to use for both studio and location photography. The more powerful and expensive units have a separate, and usually large and heavy, power unit which can be used to fire a number of individual flash-heads. This type of equipment is designed primarily for studio use where a considerable light output is required, such as in large-format still-life photography.

Choosing lighting equipment

While the choice between the different types of artificial lighting will of course be governed partly by cost, there are other considerations. Tungsten light can be less comfortable for the model when shooting portrait or glamour pictures, for example, since it is considerably brighter than the modelling lights used with electronic flash and it also generates an appreciable degree of heat. In addition, electronic flash greatly reduces the possibility of camera shake or subject movement because of the brief duriation of the flash, but on the other hand flash can be limiting in some circumstances where depth of field is an important factor, such as with still-life photographs, because the aperture selected is largely dependent on both the distance between the flash and the subject and on its power; this can sometimes make it difficult to use a small aperture for maximum depth of field unless the flash is very close to the subject, is very powerful, or you use a fast film. With tungsten lighting, of course, you can simply use a small aperture in conjunction with a longer exposure or slower shutter speed. Flash has the advantage that it can be used with daylight type film and can be combined with daylight, whereas tungsten light requires the use of artificial light film when shooting in colour and cannot be mixed with daylight without creating a colour cast. When using tungsten lighting, however, you are still able to use the TTL metering system of your camera whereas with electronic flash it is necessary to use a special flash meter (see page 110). A further advantage of studio flash units is that, unlike tungsten lighting, the power of the individual lights can be adjusted by a control switch giving a variation in light output of several stops.

Reflectors and Attachments

A light source, whether flash or tungsten, produces what is in practical terms a point source of light; this creates a sharply defined, hard-edged shadow and in most circumstances it is desirable to modify this in some way. The most basic addition to the bulb or tube is the standard dish reflector; this does little to alter the quality of the light but concentrates it more efficiently and allows it to be aimed accurately at the subject. The choice of reflector will affect the spread of light, a wide reflector covering a larger field of view and a narrow deeper shape concentrating the light into a smaller area. However, the quality of the light will only be marginally affected by the reflector itself, polished aluminium, for instance, giving a slightly harder light than a matt

A studio flash head showing the modelling lamp inside the flash tube

A conventional reflector giving an undiffused light can be used for pictures where a harder, more dramatic quality is required.

A monobloc type studio flash unit in which the power pack is contained within the flash head

white interior. It is only when the bulb or tube itself is covered in some way that the shadows it casts will be radically altered either by diffusing or reflecting its light. The open-dish reflector is used mainly for supplementary lighting when used direct, such as for illuminating the background or for rim- or back-lighting with a portrait. Its use as a main or key light is restricted to situations in which it is needed to create particularly strong modelling or a dramatic or contrasty effect – when used for a portrait, for example, it will create strong, sharply defined shadows within the model's face and will emphasize skin texture, qualities which can be both unflatter-ing and unattractive unless a specific effect is required. It is, however, effective in some circum-stances where it is important to emphasize the textural quality of a subject.

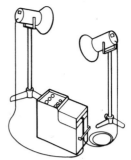

A studio flash unit with a separate power pack from which several separate heads can be fired

Normal silvered reflectors are also ideal for illuminating backgrounds where an even light tone is required.

A wide-beam reflector

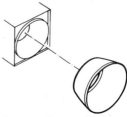

A narrow-beam reflector

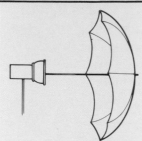

An umbrella reflector fitted to a studio flash head

An umbrella reflector is ideal for illuminating a full-length figure, as it creates quite a soft and even light when used quite close to the subject.

Umbrella reflectors

The umbrella reflector is one of the most simple and effective ways of modifying a basic light source, and also has the advantage of being portable. It is designed to fit on to the flash-head or tungsten reflector when it is aimed away from the subject so that the light is reflected back, creating a soft, diffused and evenly spread light. Umbrella reflectors are ideal as the main or key light for a portrait or for photographing a full-length figure, for example, since they will create a quite even illumination from a relatively close position. They will cast noticeable shadows though with a soft edge, giving satisfactory modelling when used at an angle of about 45° to the subject but without creating excessive contrast or with undue textural emphasis. When used from

close to the camera position an umbrella will create an almost shadowless effect within the subject and for this reason is often used for glamour or beauty lighting. The silver or gold umbrellas give a slightly harder light and with less reduction in brightness than the plain white type. Translucent white umbrellas are available and can be used as a diffuser rather than as a reflector; in this case the light is aimed at the subject and the umbrella fitted in front of it. This can give a slightly softer light, but it is important to take into account that the quality of the light is controlled largely by the size of the light source relative to the subject so that an umbrella used at some distance from the subject will create a harder light with more defined shadows than when used close to it.

A translucent umbrella can be used to diffuse the light rather than reflect it and is particularly effective for portrait and beauty photography where a soft and flattering frontal light is needed.

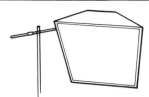

A window light provides a large source of soft, diffused light

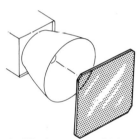

A window light is ideal for creating a large, soft, overhead light source for still life and product photography.

A diffusion screen which can be fitted in front of a conventional reflector

Window lights

These are another means of creating a soft, even spread of light. There are a number of attachments which fall into this category, with evocative names ranging from 'soft boxes' to 'fish fryers' and 'swimming-pools', but the basic principle remains the same: the light source, either a flash-tube or tungsten bulbs, is mounted within a large white rectangular reflector over which is fixed a white diffusion screen of translucent plastic, and the complete unit is usually mounted on a stand which allows it to be suspended above the subject as well as positioned vertically. This makes it ideal for still-life photography because it is a simple matter to

position the light exactly where it is needed above a set-up – indeed, this type of light is almost obligatory for food and still-life photographers. The quality of light and the precision with which it can be directed often makes any additional lights unnecessary, with only perhaps a white reflector to lighten the shadows and a spot light to create an additional highlight or two. For the same reasons it is also an ideal way of lighting beauty, fashion and glamour pictures as the quality of light it creates is very soft and flattering and its spread is so even that it can be placed quite close to the model but still giving a constant light level over a full-length figure. The same effect can be created much more cheaply, but perhaps with less convenience in use, by placing a large diffusing screen between a light with a conventional dish reflector and the subject; a wooden frame covered in tracing-paper is ideal for this purpose.

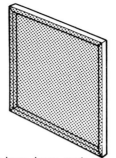

A large, home-made diffusion screen can simply be propped between the light and the subject creating a soft, even effect similar to that of a window light

Spot lights
A spot light is designed to create a very tight and concentrated beam of light, achieved by using a Fresnel lens to focus the light rays to a point at which, if required, they are almost parallel. This creates a very hard-edged shadow with dense black shadows, and is used as a key light where particularly strong emphasis is needed, to create stark dramatic shadows, for example, or to emphasize texture. A spot light is often used in portraiture, for instance, when a deliberately theatrical effect is wanted, or in food and still-life photography to reveal the subtle textures of fabrics and foods. It is a very effective way of creating additional highlights in a picture because it can be controlled so precisely, to rim-light or back-light a portrait, for instance, or to create spectacular highlights and add sparkle to a still-life picture. It can also be very useful to illuminate the background since by adjusting the focus a pool of light can be projected to create a graduation of tone on a plain background tone, adding interest and helping to separate the subject from the background. When shooting in colour, tinted acetate filters can be used over the spot light to create colour variations.

A spot light for creating a hard, narrow beam of light

Snoots and honeycombs

These are another method of controlling the spread of light, but instead of using a lens to focus the light (as with a spot light) the effect is achieved by means of a conical cowl over the light source in the case of a snoot, and by the use of horizontal slats in a honeycomb. They can be used in much the same way as a spot light but do not offer the same degree of control and give a less sharply defined shadow.

Barndoors

Barndoors are used for confining and restricting the spread of light. They consist of four movable 'flags' fitted to the front of a reflector which can be adjusted to vignette the light at the sides or top and bottom of the subject. They can be particularly useful in a small studio where light spill can be reflected indiscriminately, making the precise control of a lighting effect impossible. When using lights positioned close to the edge of the picture area, barndoors can also be very useful in preventing flare caused by the lights shining directly on to the camera lens.

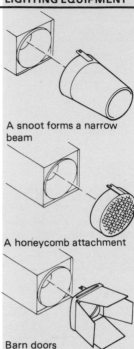

A snoot forms a narrow beam

A honeycomb attachment

Barn doors

A snoot or honeycomb is very useful for creating lighting effects.

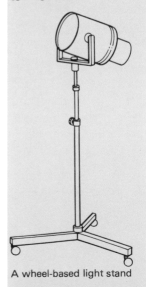

A wheel-based light stand

Lighting stands

A wide variety of different types of lighting stands is available, and the choice of the right stand for a particular purpose can make working in the studio or on location much more comfortable and convenient. The tripod-base stand is a good compromise for photographers doing both studio and location work since it can be collapsed easily for carrying and is not particularly large or heavy. The larger, wheel-based stands are more suitable for lights such as a window light, and a stand with a boom arm is vital for pictures where the light source needs to be positioned above the subject. A more elaborate system for the custom-built studio is provided by wall-mounted cantilever brackets or overhead rails which do not take up floor space. For the photographer with limited space, the sprung poles which fit between floor and ceiling take up the minimum of floor space and attachments can be bought to enable them to hold rolls of background paper too. A small low-level stand is also very useful for positioning a light behind the subject to illuminate the background, for example.

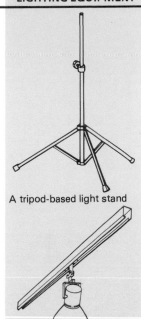

A tripod-based light stand

An overhead light rail

A light stand with a boom arm is essential where an overhead light is required.

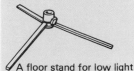

An overhead-lighting boom arm

A floor stand for low light

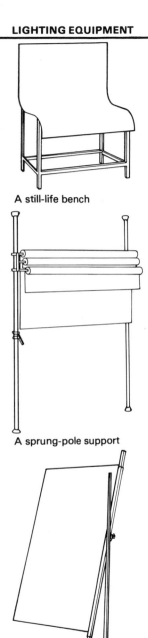

A still-life bench

A sprung-pole support

A reflector screen

Studio Accessories

There are a variety of devices and accessories that can add considerably to the convenience of working in a studio. *Tubular* construction kits are particularly helpful as they can be used to build a variety of supports either for permanent use or as and when required. A still-life bench is a great asset as it provides a surface upon which the subject can be arranged and a rail to support the background; a provision to use laminates as an alternative to paper or other fabrics is very useful and to allow a translucent plastic to be lit from underneath, for example, to create a light box. A good *background support* is also essential for the busy studio photographer who uses the large rolls of cartridge paper. These can be obtained either as brackets to fit to a wall, tripod stands or spring-loaded pole supports; up to three rolls 3 metres (10 feet) wide can be supported at once, making it quick and simple to change backgrounds.

Reflector and diffusion screens

These are standard in most studios to supplement the lighting equipment. Do-it-yourself devices using wooden frames and sheets of translucent plastic or tracing-paper and rigid white polystyrene are inexpensive and quite satisfactory, but the advantage of the manufactured accessories with collapsible aluminium frames and flexible reflective fabric is that they can be used on location.

Front projection

Front projection consists of a special projector and highly reflective screen which enables a photographer to use a colour slide as a background to a studio shot. Used judiciously, it can effectively simulate a location shot but great care is needed in setting up, and the way the subject is lit can be rather restricted. Unlike back projection which can be done with an ordinary slide projector, the special front projection equipment allows the photograph to be taken in one exposure, making it suitable for non-static subjects like fashion and glamour pictures.

Translucent, white plastic can be supported on a still-life bench and lit from underneath.

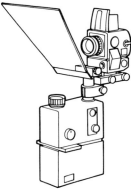

A front projection unit

Wind machines

This is a very useful piece of equipment for photographers shooting fashion, beauty and glamour pictures as it can be used to introduce a feeling of movement in a studio. It is really just a rather powerful fan with a variable speed, and can be hired from most professional dealers along with a variety of devices to create smoke effects and cobwebs.

A wind machine

Posing aids

Posing aids are a useful addition to the studio specializing in portrait photography. These are modular blocks which can be arranged to support either an individual model in a variety of positions or to make an effective and comfortable support for a group of people. Something quite similar could easily be constructed by a handiman using wooden cubes, for example, covered with plastic foam and draped with fabric.

Painted backgrounds

Painted backgrounds are widely used in professional portrait studios, to create a more interesting tonal and coloured background without the need for additional lighting which would be needed for a plain paper backdrop. The amateur photographer can achieve the same effect with a few aerosol paint sprays and a little skill.

Modular posing stools

Non-Photographic Aids

In a busy studio a large number of non-photographic aids are usually part of the standard stock of indispensable accessories. Rolls of Gaffer tape are useful for taping down stray leads and supporting lights and other accessories in inaccessible places, and generally providing a strong, firm grip which can be removed easily without damage. G-clamps are ideal for holding wooden panels together when building a small set, for instance, and a staple gun for fixing fabrics and papers. A laboratory retort stand and clamp are a good way of supporting small objects in a still-life set-up, for example, as is plasticine. Plastic beer crates can be used as a modular building block system and are strong enough to support a model on a rostrum or dias. Sheets of insulating plastic, such as rigid poly-

G clamps can be used like this to hold together a temporary structure of wall flats

Black perspex has been used in this still-life picture to provide an interesting and dramatic background.

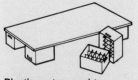

Plastic crates used to support a wooden platform

styrene foam, can be cut to make reflector screens, and perspex and laminate sheets are invaluable as backgrounds and surfaces for still-life set-ups. Domestic aluminium foil can also be used effectively as a reflective surface, and a selection of mirrors of different sizes are invaluable in still-life shots for creating small highlights. Match boxes and other small containers filled with lead shot are perfect for propping up items in a still-life arrangement and fine nylon fishing-line for suspending items that cannot be supported invisibly any other way. Tracing-paper makes a good screen for back projection and is ideal as a diffusing medium.

In addition to the accessories you can buy in photographic stores there are a variety of other items that will be a useful addition to the camera bag and can be as much a part of the basic kit of equipment as lenses and filters. A pocket recorder is invaluable for taking notes of the pictures you take, either as a record of technical information for future reference or to provide information for captions, which can be particularly important for the photographer supplying pictures for publication in books or magazines, for example, or to a picture library. A pocket torch is an asset when shooting in low-light situations, to help to set the camera controls accurately, for instance, or to find small accessories in the camera bag; it can also help in some cases to allow you to focus more accurately when the ambient light is very poor and with long exposures it can be used effectively to 'paint' foreground details with light in order to give additional detail.

A multi-purpose knife like the Swiss Army model is something that many experienced photographers would not be without; apart from the usefulness of a sharp blade it has a saw edge for removing unwanted foliage, for example, screwdrivers for changing plugs in foreign hotels, tweezers for removing jammed polaroids or film inadvertently wound back into the cassette, and a magnifying glass for checking the focus as well as a means of opening bottles and cans. Other useful items include a roll of sticky tape, a marking-pen for labelling exposed films and a black plastic bag to keep them in.

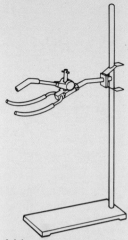

A laboratory retort stand and clamp

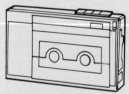

A pocket recorder

A pocket torch

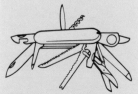

A Swiss army knife

Equipment Glossary

Categories
1 Family Record
2 People
3 Landscape
4 Action
5 Studio and Professional
6 Specialist and Nature

Bold numbers identify the best use for each item.

Accessory shoe 1–4, **1** A device attached to the camera body which enables a variety of accessories to be fitted directly on to it, such as a flash-gun or separate viewfinder. See Hot shoe.

Adapter ring 1–6 A metal ring with a different-sized thread at each end which allows a filter or other attachment to be interchanged on different-sized lens mounts.

Aperture priority 1–6, **3** An automatic metering system within a camera in which the selected aperture is set manually and the camera automatically selects the shutter speed according to the brightness level and the film speed.

Artificial light film 1 2 4 5 6, **1, 4** Colour transparency film which is balanced for correct colour when used with a light source of either 3200° Kelvin or 3400° Kelvin.

Autofocus 1 2 4 5 6, **1, 4** A motor-driven mechanism which automatically sets the camera lens to the correct focus in response to a signal transmitted from the camera and reflected from the subject, or by measurement of image contrast.

Automatic aperture 1–6 An iris diaphragm, or lens aperture, mechanism which remains wide open for focusing and viewing but stops down automatically to a pre-set aperture when the shutter is fired.

Automatic exposure control 1–6, **1, 4** A system whereby an exposure meter is coupled to the camera settings and controls either or both the shutter speed and aperture to give the right combination for correct exposure according to the brightness level and the film speed.

Background rolls 2 5 6, **5** Specially made wide rolls of cartridge paper in a wide range of colours used to provide a seamless backdrop for photographs.

Background unit 2 5 6, **5** Equipment designed for supporting background rolls in the form of either wall-mounted brackets, tripod-based stands or spring-loaded poles.

Back-light button 1–4 6, **1** A device fitted to some cameras with automatic exposure control which gives one and a half or two stops extra exposure, for use with subjects where the light is behind them.

Back projection 5 6, **5** A set-up using a slide projector and a translucent screen which allows a colour transparency to be used as the background for a subject.

Bag bellows 3 5 6, **5** Special wide non-concertina-type bellows which are used on view cameras to allow a short focal length to be used and to permit the full use of camera movements.

Ball and socket head 1–6 An adjustable top for a tripod or other camera support which allows the camera to be tilted and locked at any angle.

Barndoors 5 6, **5** An attachment for a photographic light which allows the spread of light to be controlled by the means of four adjustable flaps.

Baseboard camera 3 5 6, **5** A large-format camera in which the lens panel and the film back are supported on a baseboard making it easy to collapse and set up and therefore more portable than a monorail camera but with fewer movements.

B or bulb setting 1–6 Shutter speed setting which allows the shutter to be held open for as long as the shutter release is depressed, for use when exposures longer than those marked on the shutter speed dial are required.

Bellows unit 5 6, 6 An adjustable light-tight flexible sleeve which fits between the camera body and the lens to allow focusing at very close distances for close-up and macro photography.

Between-the-lens shutter 1–3 5 6 A shutter mechanism positioned within the elements of a camera lens; its advantage is that it can be synchronized with electronic flash at all speeds but it has a limited top speed of about 1/500 sec.

Boom stand 5 6, 5 A light stand with a counter-balanced horizontal arm which can be adjusted to suspend a light directly above the subject.

Box camera 1–3, 1 Simple camera with limited control over focusing and exposure.

Brightline viewfinder 1–6, 1, 4 Direct-vision viewfinder in which the subject is seen surrounded by a bright frame superimposed over the image, often with additional lines for lenses of different focal length and to show the allowance needed for parallax error when the subject is close to the camera.

Bulk film 2–6, 4 35 mm film supplied in long rolls as opposed to cassettes for use in special film backs or for self-loading into cassettes for economy.

Cable release 1–6 Flexible cable which is attached to the camera's shutter release to allow it to be activated without direct pressure on the camera body, used for slow shutter speeds and time exposures when the camera is mounted on a tripod; extra long versions can be used for self-portraits and remote control.

Camera movements 5 6, 5 Means of adjusting position and angle of the lens

panel and film holder for large-format cameras to give control over depth of field and perspective.

Cartridge 1–6, 1 Method of supplying film which is pre-loaded into a light-tight container and can be loaded directly into the camera without the need for threading as with a 35 mm cassette or a rollfilm.

Cartridge camera 1–4, 1 A camera which is designed to use pre-loaded film cartridges exclusively, such as 110 or instant picture, the disadvantage is that a more limited choice of film types are available.

Cassette 1–6 A light-tight container in which film is supplied to allow daylight loading of the camera without the need for backing paper as with a rollfilm, for example. Most normal cassettes are disposable but it is possible to buy reusable versions for bulk loading.

Catadioptric lens 2–4 6, 4 6 A long-focal-length lens which uses a mirror within the optical system to make the lens more compact than a conventional design would allow; it usually has a fixed aperture. Also known as a mirror or reflex lens.

CC filters 1–6, 5 Colour conversion filters, usually supplied as acetate squares which are used to correct an imbalance between the colour temperature of the light source and that for which the film is balanced. They are available in both the primary and complementary colours in a wide range of strengths from very pale to saturated.

Changing bag 2–6 Light-tight bag with arm-holes which allows film to be handled without a darkroom for the purpose of loading darkslides, for example, or a daylight developing tank.

Click stops 1–6 Positive 'locked' settings on the aperture ring of a lens which allow the aperture to be set accurately in intervals of one, half or one-third of a stop without the need for visual alignment.

Clip test 2–6 Method of taking a short piece of film from the end of a roll for processing, so that the remainder of the film can have a modified development if any exposure or contrast correction is needed.

Close-up attachments 5 6, 6 A general term to describe accessories that allow a lens to be focused at a closer distance than its marked minimum setting; it includes bellows units, extension tubes and close-up lenses.

Coated lens 1–6 A lens that has an anti-reflection treatment applied to the glass-to-air surfaces to prevent flare, increase light transmission and image contrast; most modern lenses are now coated.

Colour balancing filters 1–6 Filters that adjust the difference in colour balance between a specific light source and the film in use.

Colour compensation filters 1–6 Another term used to describe filters which are used to prevent a colour cast as the result of a difference between the colour temperature of the light source and the film in use.

Colour temperature meter 5, 6 An instrument for measuring the colour temperature of a light source to determine the exact filtration needed to correct a colour cast.

Compact camera 1–4, 1 Term used to describe a relatively simple camera with a fixed lens using 35 mm or cartridge film, usually with a direct-vision viewfinder.

Contrast filters 1–6, 3 A term used to describe coloured filters used with black-and-white film to create contrast between objects of a similar tone but of a different colour in a scene.

Converter lens 1–6 A supplementary lens which is used to alter the focal length of the lens to which it is attached in order to give a wider or narrower field of view.

Correction filter 1–6 A term used to describe a filter used to alter the films response to an image in order to create a more natural or pleasing effect.

Coupled exposure meter 1–6 An exposure meter built into the camera which is linked to either or both of the aperture or shutter controls so that a visual indication is given when they are set to give the correct exposure.

Coupled rangefinder 1–6 A method of accurate focusing for cameras without a focusing screen such as a viewfinder camera; the focus is adjusted until two separate images of the subject merge together at the correct setting.

Darkcloth 3 5 6, 5 Black fabric cloth which is used to surround the viewing screen and the photographer's head to make it easier to see the image by excluding extraneous light.

Darkslide 3 5 6, 5 Light-tight container holding one sheet of film on each side covered by a protective slide which is withdrawn after the slide has been placed in the back of a large-format camera prior to exposure.

Daylight colour film 1–6 Colour film manufactured to give correct colour balance at a colour temperature of about 5500° Kelvin equal to that of noon sunlight, electronic flash and blue-tinted flashbulbs.

Dedicated flash 1 2 4–6, 1, 4 A flash-gun with an automatic exposure control which is coupled to the TTL metering system of a particular make of camera.

Delayed action 1–6, 1 A device connected to the shutter release mechanism of a camera which allows a delay of up to 10 sec or more after the shutter release has been depressed before firing the shutter; useful for self-portraits and time exposures when a cable release is not available.

Depth of field scale 1–6 A scale engraved on the focusing mount of a lens which indicates the depth of field obtained at any combination of aperture and focusing distance.

Diaphragm 1–6 The name given to an adjustable lens aperture to control the amount of light passing through the lens, also called an iris.

Diffraction grating 1–6 Lens attachment which creates rainbow-coloured bands of light around highlights and bright areas of an image by the means of a grid of fine lines engraved into its surface. Also called a colourburst filter.

Diffuser 1 2 5 6, 5 A white translucent fabric which is used in front of a light source to diffuse it, creating a softer light with less defined shadows.

Diffusion filter 1–6, 2 A clear glass or plastic filter which has an engraved surface to diffuse the image creating a soft-focus effect.

Direct-vision viewfinder 1–6, 1, 4 A means of aiming and framing a camera which does not have a viewing screen; it uses a separate optical system to that of the camera lens.

Distance symbols 1–4, 1 A graphic means of focusing for a simple camera in which the lens is set to a head-and-shoulders shape for 1–2 metres (3–6 feet), half-length figure for 2–3 metres (6–9 feet), full-length figure for 3–6 metres (9–20 feet) and a mountain for distances of 6 metres (20 feet) to infinity.

Dolly 5 6, 5 A separate wheel base which can be attached to a tripod-based light or camera stand for easy movement in the studio.

Double extension 5 6, 5 A facility for large-format cameras which enables the bellows to be extended to twice the distance of the focal length of the standard lens giving a 1:1 image-to-subject ratio for close-up photography.

Edge numbers 1–6 Pre-exposed numbers along the edge of film allowing a reference to be made to a particular frame after development.

Electronic flash 1–6 Artificial lighting which uses a capacitor to store up an electric charge and releases it into a gas-filled tube, unlike flash bulbs or cubes, giving a very large number of flashes.

Electronic shutter 1–6 A battery-operated shutter in which the exposures are timed by electronic means as opposed to mechanical.

Ever-ready case 1–3, 1 A camera case in which the front drops down or can be removed allowing pictures to be taken without the need to take the camera from its case.

Expiry date 1–6 The date marked on a pack of film which indicates the maximum recommended time it should be kept before use; however, storage conditions can both extend and reduce this time.

Exposure meter 1–6 An instrument which uses an electrical current to measure the brightness level of a subject or light source; it can be a separate hand-held accessory or built into the camera and coupled to the aperture and shutter mechanisms to give automatic or semi-automatic control.

Extension tubes 5 6, 6 A means of increasing the lens-to-film distance in order to allow focusing at closer distances than the minimum setting marked on the lens, consisting of a number of tubes of different thicknesses which can be fitted singly or in combination between the camera body and lens; some allow the auto-iris and exposure control of the camera to be maintained.

Fast lens 1–6, 4 A lens which has a wide maximum aperture for its focal length giving a bright image on the screen of an SLR camera and allowing pictures to be taken more easily in poor lighting conditions.

Field camera 3 5 6, **3, 5** A term used to describe a large-format camera which uses a baseboard to support the lens and film plane panels as opposed to a monorail. Also called a view camera.

Fill-in 2 5 6, **5** A term used to describe a light or reflector which is used to add light to the shadow areas of a subject in order to show more detail and to reduce contrast.

Film pack 1–6 A means by which sheet film can be loaded into a camera and exposed in succession without the need for a darkroom or additional slides. Also the method by which most instant films are packed.

Film speed 1–6 The means by which the relative sensitivity of different films is measured and used to determine the correct exposure for a specific brightness level. It is widely expressed as an ISO number in which ISO 100/21 is twice the speed of ISO 50/18 and half the speed of ISO 200/24.

Filter 1–6 A transparent glass, plastic or gelatin attachment which is placed over a lens or a light source to prevent some of the wavelengths of light from passing.

Filter factor 1–6 The amount by which the exposure must be increased to compensate for the use of a particular filter: the exposure for a filter with a factor of × 2, for example, must be doubled or increased by one stop.

Fish-eye lens 1–6, **5, 6** An extreme wide-angle lens giving a field of view of 180° or more by allowing straight lines to become progressively more curved the further they are from the centre of the image.

Fixed-focus lens 1–4, **1** A lens on a simple camera which is set permanently to the hyperfocal distance; this is the optimum distance at which the depth of field will record both near and distant details with acceptable sharpness.

Flash 1–6 An artificial light source which uses either an expendable bulb or a reusable gas-filled tube which are triggered electronically to produce a brief but very bright burst of light.

Flashbulb 1–6 See Flash.

Flash factor 1–6 A method of calculating exposure when using flash. A number related to a particular flash-gun or bulb and film speed is divided by the distance it is from the subject to give the correct aperture.

Flash synchronization 1–6 Device within the camera shutter which triggers a connected flash-gun at the precise moment the shutter is fully open. The X setting is used for electronic flash and the M setting for flashbulbs, the difference being that flash is instantaneous but bulbs take a fraction of a second longer to reach full brightness and must be triggered sooner.

Flood light 1 2 5 6, **5** An artificial light source with a wide reflector that produces a broad spread of light over a wide area.

F-number 1–6 The method by which the aperture scale is marked. The number is arrived at by dividing the focal length of the lens by the diameter of the aperture; each increment of a larger number reduces the light passing through the lens by half, and each smaller number doubles the amount of light, e.g. f8 is half f5.6 and f2.8 is double f4.

Focal length 1–6 The distance between the film plane and the lens when it is focused at infinity.

Focal plane shutter 1–6, **4** A shutter which is incorporated into the camera body using a variable slit which travels across the film plane at a variable speed according to the exposure set. It has the advantage of having a faster top speed than a between-the-lens shutter and makes extra lenses cheaper.

Focusing hood 1–6 A device for shielding extraneous light from the viewing screen of a camera to aid viewing and focusing.

Focusing magnifier 1–6 A device for magnifying the image on a viewing screen to aid accurate focusing.

Focusing scale 1–6 A distance scale marked on the focusing mount of a lens.

Focusing screen 1–6, **5** A translucent glass or plastic plate positioned at the film plane to enable the image formed by the camera lens to be viewed and focused.

Format 1–6 The size and proportion of a particular film or paper or the image area of a particular camera.

Front projection 4–6, **5** Studio equipment using a special projector and a highly reflective screen to allow a colour transparency to be used as a background.

Gelatin filter 1–6 Thin flexible filter which is available in an extremely wide range of colours and types.

Graduated filter 1–6 A filter in which the tint is only applied to part of the filter leaving the remainder clear.

Grey card 5 6, **6** Special tinted card of 18 per cent grey which is used for exposure measurement in critical work. It represents the mid-tone in an image for which exposure meters are calibrated.

Guide number 1–6 Method of determining flash exposures; see Flash factor.

Half-frame 1–4, **1** 35 mm camera designed to produce 72 pictures on a standard cassette of 36 exposures (or 40 on a 20-exposure cassette) with an image size of 18×24 mm, half the normal 24×36 mm.

Half-plate 5 6 Film format of early large-format plate cameras taking pictures 6½×4¾ inches in size.

Hot shoe 1–6, **1** Accessory shoe on a camera which provides an electrical contact for a flash-gun, making a synchronization cable unnecessary.

Ideal format 2–6 Term used to describe an 'ideal' proportion for a picture of 4:3, it

usually refers to the 6×9 cm format of some rollfilm cameras, but can be equally applied to those producing 6×4.5cm.

Incident light attachment 2–6, **5** An attachment for an exposure meter which allows it to measure the brightness of a light source as well as that reflected from the subject.

Infra-red focus 3 5 6, **6** A setting on the focusing mount of some lenses which allows for the fact that infra-red light rays are focused at a slightly different point from those of visible light.

Instamatic camera 1–3, **1** Trade name and generic term for a simple camera using the 126 film cartridge.

Instant picture camera 1–6, **1** Camera exclusively for use with instant film.

Interchangeable lens 1–6 Facility with many types of camera which allows the lens to be detached and for others of different focal length to be fitted.

Iris diaphragm 1–6 See Diaphragm.

ISO 1–6 Stands for International Standards Organization and is used as a measurement of film speed incorporating the DIN and ASA indexes.

Joule 2 4 5 6, **5** Unit of measurement used to express the power of an electronic flash. A joule is equal to one watt-second or to 40 lumen-seconds.

Kelvin 2–6 Unit of measurement used to express the colour temperature of a light source. It is the temperature in degrees Kelvin to which an inert substance must be heated to emit light of a specific colour.

Key light 2 5 6, **5** The term used to describe the dominant light source in an image.

Large-format camera 2 3 5 6, **5** Term used to describe cameras using sheet film.

LCD 1–6 Stands for Liquid Crystal Display and is a method commonly used to display exposure and other information in the viewfinder of a camera.

Leaf shutter 1–6 See Between-the-lens shutter.

LED 1–6 Stands for Light Emitting Diodes and is a commonly used method of displaying exposure and other information in the viewfinder of a camera and also warning signals for potential operator errors.

Lens cap 1–6 Protective covers for the front and back elements of a lens.

Lens hood 1–6 Attachment which fits on the front of a lens to shield it from extraneous light which might cause flare.

Light meter 1–6 An alternative term for an exposure meter.

Light tent 5 6, 5 Structure made of white translucent material used to surround a subject when a soft shadowless light is needed or to avoid reflections in polished surfaces.

Long-focus lens 1–6 A term used to describe a lens which has a substantially greater focal length than the diagonal measurement of the film format it is being used with, creating a narrower field of view.

Macro attachment 5–6 Supplementary lens used in conjunction with a normal lens to allow it to focus at a closer distance than indicated on the focusing mount.

Macro lens 5–6, 6 A specially computed lens designed to focus at a distance which allows a 1:1 subject-to-image ratio and gives optimum performances at close focusing distances.

Microprism 1–6 A focusing aid incorporated into the viewing screen.

Miniature camera 1–6 Term coined originally to describe the 35 mm camera, and now only applied to very small cameras.

Mirror lens 2–6 See Catadiaoptric lens.

Mode 1–6 Term used to describe the system selected in an automatic camera.

Modelling light 2 4 5 6, 5 A tungsten bulb incorporated into an electronic flash unit to allow the effect of the lighting to be assessed visually.

Monorail camera 5 6, 5 A large-format sheet-film camera of modular design in which the lens panel and film plane are supported on a single rail, with the advantage of allowing a wide range of camera movements.

Motor drive 2 4 5 6, 4 An attachment which allows the film to be advanced automatically and automatic firing in rapid sequence. It is powered by batteries or nickel cadmium rechargeable cells.

Motor wind 1–6, 4 Available both as an attachment and in many cases built into the camera; it allows automatic film advance and sequential firing at a less rapid rate than a motor drive.

Multimode camera 1–6 A camera which offers a choice of operating modes, such as aperture priority, shutter priority, manual or programmed.

Multiple exposure button 1–6 A device which allows the double exposure prevention mechanism fitted to most cameras be to be bypassed permitting deliberate multiple exposures for effect.

Multiple flash 2 4 5 6 A lighting arrangement using more than one flash unit, or the technique of making a number of exposures with a single flash on the same piece of film.

Neutral density filter 1–6 A grey filter in a range of densities used to reduce the brightness of the image on the film in precise increments.

Open flash 1–6 The technique used in multiple flash of holding the shutter open on a time exposure and firing the flash-gun manually.

Pan and tilt head 1–6 Adjustable top for a tripod or other camera support which allows independent control of the horizontal and vertical movements.

Panoramic camera 2–6, **3**, **6** Specially designed camera which uses a swivelling lens to produce an extremely wide field of view without distortion, giving a picture of elongated proportions.

Parallax lines 1–6 The indication in the viewfinder of non-SLR or view cameras which allows for the difference in viewpoint and the corresponding field of view that is caused by the viewfinder lens being in a different position to the camera lens. This is most noticeable at close focusing distances.

Pentaprism 1–6 A five-sided prism used to allow the image on the viewing screen of an SLR camera to be seen at eye-level. It also reverses the laterally reversed image on the screen to its normal appearance.

Photoflood ·1–6, **5** An artificial light source designed for photography similar to a domestic bulb but 'over-run' to give a higher output with a much shorter life.

Photomicrography 5 6, **6** Method of taking photographs through a microscope; some SLR system cameras have the attachments available in their range of accessories.

Pinhole camera 1–6 Method of taking photographs with an image formed by a minute hole instead of a lens.

Polarizing filter 1–6 A neutral grey filter which can be used to eliminate polarized light from a subject when it is reflected from a non-metallic surface.

Polaroid camera 1–6, **1** Both the trade name and a generic term for a camera designed to use instant picture film.

Process lens 5 6, **6** A specially designed lens for large-format cameras and reproduction equipment to give the highest quality image of flat artwork and lettering, used mainly in printing industry.

Pulling 1–6 A term used to describe the technique of modifying development times in order to reduce the speed of a film.

Pushing 1–6 The opposite to pulling; to increase the speed of a film.

Rangefinder 1–6 A means of measuring the distance of a subject optically; it is often coupled to the focusing mechanism of viewfinder cameras.

Reflex cameras 1–6 A term used to describe a camera which uses a mirror to deflect the image from a lens up on to a viewing screen.

Reflex lens 2–6 See Catadioptric lens.

Reversal film 1–6 Film which produces a positive image during processing, without the need for a separate negative.

Ring flash 5 6, **6** A flash-gun with a tube designed to fit around the lens giving an even, shadowless light, used mainly for close-up photography.

Rising front 5 6, **5** A facility on a view camera which allows the optical axis of the lens to be raised to control perspective.

Rollfilm back 2 3 5 6, **5** An accessory for a large-format camera which enables rollfilm to be used as well as sheet film.

Scrim 5 6, **5** An attachment for a studio light which reduces its brightness without affecting its colour quality.

Shutter priority 1–6, **4** An automatic exposure metering system for a camera which allows the user to set the shutter speed manually while the camera sets the aperture according to the brightness level and the speed of the film in use.

Single lens reflex (SLR) 1–6, **6** A camera which uses a mirror to deflect the image from the lens up on to a viewing screen.

Skylight filter 1–6 Pale warm-tinted filter designed to reduce blue casts on colour film due to UV light and haze.

Slave unit 1–6, **5** Photoelectric cell which is connected to a flash-gun so that it can be triggered simultaneously from the flash of another gun without the need for a connecting cable.

Snoot 5 6, **5** A device for restricting the spread of light from a studio light.

Soft-focus attachment 1–6 See Diffusion.

Spot Meter 5 6, **6** A studio light which uses a lens to give a concentrated beam of light creating a hard-edged shadow.

Standard lens 1–6 A lens which has a focal length similar to the diagonal measurement of the film format with which it is used.

Stereo camera 1–6, **1** A camera which uses two or more lenses to create an image which can give the illusion of three-dimensions on a flat two-dimensional print.

Strobe light 5 6, **5** An electronic light source which can be used to flash rapidly at controlled intervals; also a trade name and generic term for studio flash equipment.

Supplementary lens 1–6 A lens which is attached to a prime lens in order to alter its focal length.

Swing back/front 5 6, **5** Facilities on a large format camera which can be used to control perspective and depth of field.

Technical camera 5 6, **5** Term used to describe a large-format baseboard camera.

Telephoto lens 1–6 A long-focus lens using optical elements to make it more compact.

Thyristor flash-gun 1–6, **1, 4** A flash-gun with automatic exposure control, which uses a light sensor to control the duration of the flash according to the aperture and speed of the film in use. It also helps to conserve power and speed up recycling.

Tri-colour filters 5 6, **6** A set of three filters in the primary colours, red, green and blue, used for making colour separations in reproduction processes, also with creative applications.

Tripod 1–6 Collapsible three-legged camera support, also base for portable lighting stands.

T-setting 1–6 A setting on the shutter speed dial of a camera which allows the shutter to be opened with one depression of the release and remaining so until depressed again.

TTL 1–6 Stands for through-the-lens metering and is an exposure metering system in which light-sensitive cells within the camera body take a reading from the image created by the camera lens.

Twin lens reflex 1–6 A camera which uses a separate lens from that which exposes the film to create an image on a viewing screen with the aid of a mirror.

UV filter 1–6 A filter which reduces the blue cast created by ultra-violet light.

View camera 3 5 6, **3, 5** A large-format camera using sheet film in which viewing and focusing are carried out on a ground-glass screen at the film plane.

Viewfinder 1–6 An optical device which shows the field of view given by a particular lens or camera.

Whole plate camera 5 6, **5** Large-format camera using a film format of 6½ × 8½ inches.

Wide-angle lens 1–6 A lens which has a focal length substantially less than the diagonal measurement of the film format in use, giving a wider field of view than a standard lens.

Zone system 3 5 6, **6** A method of exposure determination which uses a precise series of tones in the subject related to negative and print densities so that both exposure and development can be controlled to give a pre-determined effect when using individual sheets of film.

Zoom lens 1–6 A lens with a continuously variable focal length and corresponding field of view within a given range.

Film Guide

A list of currently available films would be of little lasting value since film technology is advancing rapidly and changes and improvements are taking place at frequent intervals. However, the general principles involved in both choosing and using film remain much the same and this guide is intended to help the photographer in doing this rather than to give an itemized list.

Black-and-white film

Films for normal use are of the panchromatic type, which means that they are equally sensitive to all visible wavelengths of light, recording a subject in terms of its different brightness levels. However, some specialized black-and-white films are designed to respond more to particular parts of the spectrum and these can also be used for creative effects. *Infra-red film*, for example, is particularly sensitive to the invisible infra-red radiation and when used with an infra-red filter or with a deep red filter will give unusual and dramatic tonal renderings of a subject, with green foliage recording as nearly white, for example, and blue skies as black. *Orthochromatic film* is not sensitive to reds and will record colours at this end of the spectrum as a very dark or black tone on the print. *Lith film* is designed to record an image only in terms of black-and-white, eliminating mid-tones, and can be used to create dramatic high-contrast effects. It is also possible to obtain black-and-white film that will give a direct positive image during processing. Specialized films of this type are only available in certain formats, usually 35 mm and sheet film.

The main consideration with normal negative films is speed. The speed of a film is directly linked to the grain size and this in turn affects the definition and quality of a image. For subjects where sharpness and image quality are the most important factors it is sensible to use the slowest film that is practicable according to the subject and the lighting conditions. Even in poor light if the subject is static and the camera can be mounted on a tripod to allow a slow shutter speed to be used, a slow, fine-grained film can still be used. However, where there is subject movement to consider and a fast shutter speed must be used, then it will be necessary to select a faster film. Film format and the degree of enlargement are also important factors in this respect – an 8×10 print from a rollfilm negative will show little grain and produce high image quality even with a fast film, whereas a 16×20 inch enlargement from a slow, fine-grained 35 mm negative will inevitably show some grain. Grain should not necessarily always be considered an undesirable quality, indeed the slight grittiness of a 35 mm photograph is often an inherent part of its appeal when applied to an appropriate subject such as reportage, and in many cases grain can be deliberately increased to create a pictorial effect. When this is done it is best to select a very fast film, possibly uprating it with push-processing to enhance it further and to compose the image so that it can be cropped and enlarged to a greater degree to obtain the maximum effect of the grain.

Colour films

There are two main types of colour film – colour transparency and colour negative – and within these categories there are very many different makes and types. Colour transparency film is designed to produce a direct positive image during processing and is the best choice when slides are needed for reproduction in books or magazines, for example. If a colour print is the prime requisite, however, then colour negative film is the best choice; although it is possible to make colour prints from transparencies they tend to be more expensive than prints made from negatives, and the cheaper machine-made prints tend to be of higher quality when made from negatives. Colour negative film also has a wider exposure latitude than transparency materials and is more suitable for inexperienced photographers and those with a simple camera as it will still give an acceptable result even with a considerable degree of exposure error. On the other hand, a photographer who wants to make his own colour prints may well find it easier to do so from transparencies than from colour negatives as the process has more latitude with exposure and filtration and it is easier to judge print quality when you can compare it with the original transparency, whereas a colour negative bears little resemblance to the original subject.

The same considerations concerning film speed and image quality apply to colour films as to black-and-white: slow films produce a sharper, less grainy image than faster films, and like black-and-white films the speed rating of colour films can also be changed by modified processing. Colour casts caused by the light source being of a different colour temperature from that for which the film is balanced can be corrected to a large extent at the printing stage in the case of colour negative film, so the same type of film can be used under different lighting conditions; when the subject requires longer exposures, however, a special type L negative film is recommended. Some amateur photographers are tempted to use the professional type colour negative film thinking that it will give better results, but it is not suitable for use in the processing and automatic printing equipment used for inexpensive enprinting and will in fact give inferior results. Unlike colour negative film, the transparency materials are balanced for use in a light source of specific colour temperature and day-light film should only be used in daylight or with electronic flash. Artificial light type film must be used with tungsten or halogen lighting, although colour conversion filters can be used if the correct film is not available. In mixed lighting conditions it is best to use the film that is balanced for the pre-dominant light source.

Bibliography

Abring, H. D., *Von Daguerre Bis Heute*
(Herausgeber Privates Foto-Museum,
1981/82)

Angel, Heather, *The Book of Close Up Photography*
(Ebury Press, 1983)

Busselle, Michael, *The Encyclopaedia of
Photography* (Octopus Books, 1983)
Master Photography (Mitchell Beazley, 1977)
Nude and Glamour Photography (Macdonald,
1981)
Photographing People (Macdonald, 1980)

Coe, Brian, *Cameras* (Marshall Cavendish, 1978)

Freeman, Michael, *The Studio Manual* (Collins,
1984)
Wildlife and Nature Photography (Croom
Helm, 1981)

Garrett, John and Calder, Julien, *The 35mm
Photographer's Handbook* (Pan Books, 1979)

Goldsmith, Arthur, *The Camera and Its Images*
(Newsweek Books, 1979)

Hedgecoe, John, *The Photographer's Handbook*
(Ebury Press, 1979)

Langford, Michael, *Complete Encyclopaedia of
Photography* (Ebury Press, 1982)
Special Effects Photography (Ebury Press,
1981)

Pinkard, Bruce, *The Photographer's Dictionary*
(Batsford, 1982)

Time Life Library of Photography (Time Life Books,
1981)

Index

Acknowledgements

The author would like to express his thanks to the following people: John Miller for the photographs on pages 67, 173 and 174 and for his assistance and help with black-and-white printing; Don Wood for the photograph on page 160; Julien Busselle for help in the studio and darkroom; Hilary Dickinson for editing the text; Martin Atcherley for designing the book; and Daniella Gluck for guiding it all to completion.